D1243396

Claas Junghans, Adam Levy
Intellectual Property
Management

Related Titles

Ebel, H. F., Bliefert, C., Russey, W. E.

The Art of Scientific Writing

From Student Reports to Professional Publications in Chemistry and Related Fields

2004
Softcover
ISBN 3-527-29829-0

Bamfield, P.

Research and Development Management in the Chemical and Pharmaceutical Industry

2003
Hardcover
ISBN 3-527-30667-6

Jakobi, R.

Marketing and Sales in the Chemical Industry

2002
Hardcover
ISBN 3-527-30625-0

Hansen, B., Hirsch, F.

Protecting Inventions in Chemistry

Commentary on Chemical Case Law under the European Patent Convention and the German Patent Law

1997
Hardcover
ISBN 3-527-28808-2

Budde, F., Felcht, U.-H., Frankemölle, H. (Eds.)

Value Creation

Strategies for the Chemical Industry

Second, Completely Revised and Extended Edition
2006
Hardcover
ISBN 3-527-31266-8

Claas Junghans, Adam Levy

Intellectual Property Management

A Guide for Scientists, Engineers, Financiers, and Managers

With Contributions By
Rolf Sander, Tobias Boeckh, Jan Dirk Heerma,
and Christoph Regierer

WILEY-
VCH

WILEY-VCH Verlag GmbH & Co. KGaA

Authors

Dr. Claas Junghans
Oldenburger Str. 37
10551 Berlin
Germany

Adam Levy
4 Birchencliffe Cottages
Pott Shrigley
Cheshire
SK10 5SE
UK

Dr. Rolf Sander
Stapel Rechtsanwälte
Marburger Str. 3
10789 Berlin
Germany

Dr. Tobias Boeckh
HERTIN Anwaltssozietät
Kurfürstendamm 54–55
10707 Berlin
Germany

Dr. Jan Dirk Heerma
SJ Berwin LLP
Kurfürstendamm 63
10707 Berlin
Germany

Dr. Christoph Regierer
Dr. Röver und Partner KG
Auguste-Viktoria-Str. 118
14193 Berlin
Germany

Library of Congress Card No.: applied for
British Library Cataloguing-in-Publication Data
A catalogue record for this book is available from the British Library.

**Bibliographic information published by
Die Deutsche Bibliothek**
Die Deutsche Bibliothek lists this publication in the Deutsche Nationalbibliografie; detailed bibliographic data is available in the Internet at <http://dnb.ddb.de>.

© 2006 WILEY-VCH Verlag GmbH & Co. KGaA, Weinheim

Printed in the Federal Republic of Germany.
Printed on acid-free paper.

Typesetting   Kühn & Weyh, Satz und Medien, Freiburg
Printing   betz-druck GmbH, Darmstadt
Bookbinding   Litges & Dopf Buchbinderei GmbH, Heppenheim

ISBN-13:   978-3-527-31286-3
ISBN-10:   3-527-31286-2

Contents

Intellectual Property Management. Claas Junghans, Adam Levy
Copyright © 2006 WILEY-VCH Verlag GmbH & Co. KGaA, Weinheim

Preface

To the uninitiated, the world of intellectual property often appears an impenetrable collision of legal, scientific and economic themes. Indeed, the study of intellectual property draws from these three disciplines in a way that our educational and philosophical systems struggle to reconcile. Technically-expert lawyers, scientists and economists find it equally difficult to adopt a holistic overview and to look beyond their specialised field.

Whilst Patent Offices have recently intensified their efforts to be more accessible, publishing readable introductions to the very basic terms of intellectual property, and guides to initial patent application, these laudable efforts fail to penetrate the heart of the problem as we see it: the connection of legal procedure, beyond its mere application, with technological development and the business strategy that drives it.

"Intellectual Property Management" provides an introduction to the world of creating value through inventions. This book is written by international experts who from their day-to-day experience are able to position the technical and legal nature of patents within an economic and commercial framework. Readers are given a clear view of patents as a rational business process, and are presented with a toolbox with which to make careful assessment of the time and money that inventions warrant, concentrating on an assessment of risk, and within this framework, on maximising both value and personal return. From these carefully elaborated fundamental principles, we progress to address more complex and sophisticated issues of intellectual property strategic planning and wider corporate strategy.

The first four chapters of this book treat the aspects of patenting that both an inventor and a manager of an invention-intensive business will need to understand to make meaningful decisions on the subject. In doing so, the authors have concentrated on the underlying principles of the process, which are similar to almost all countries, rather than on precise definition of local regulations. Indeed, readers may note a certain European bias in the book. The European Patent Convention is both the largest judicial entity in the world of IP, and its law, in its synthesis of both Anglo-Saxon and French-German legal influences, presents a paradigm for most other patent systems in this world. The great exception to this rule is the USA, which treats many problems differently from all other systems.

Intellectual Property Management. Claas Junghans, Adam Levy
Copyright © 2006 WILEY-VCH Verlag GmbH & Co. KGaA, Weinheim

Important differences are highlighted wherever necessary. Moreover, where easily readable literature exists in the English language on patenting, it is likely to concentrate on the US system, and the reader desiring to learn specifically about this system will find literature easily. Nevertheless, we hope that such readers will benefit from our specific treatment of the economic perspective.

Chapter 1, "Terminology", defines the patent landscape, providing an elementary terminology and foundation upon which the reminder of the book builds. Readers already familiar with the world of patents may refer to this chapter as reference whenever needed.

Chapter 2, "The Economic Objectives of Patenting", sets the economic framework in which patents reside, with an emphasis on the formulation of a basic patent strategy and a comprehensive explanation of patent routes and of patent scope and claim breadth. The authors have debated extensively the position of this chapter within the book. We have finally opted for moving it before the technical chapters on patenting, authorship and licensing. This position follows our conviction that in order to make a meaningful use of the legal tools that IP offers, one must define the economic objectives that drive the patenting process. All too often, resources are spent unwisely because the applicants did not consider their motives in submitting the application until far into the patenting process.

Chapter 3, "Patenting", is the most technical chapter of the book. It discusses patent searching, drafting and application, and at what point, and how, to hire an attorney. The chapter concludes with an explanation of patent strategy in a dynamic research environment, and the exploitation of patent families. It must be emphasized that this book does not pretend to be a "do-it-yourself" guide to successful patent applications. Although there are cases where inventors have successfully patented and marketed their inventions, we do not encourage the reader to do so. Nevertheless, the cost and satisfaction of collaborating with a professional patent attorney can, in our view, often be improved substantially if the client, the inventor or applicant, has a good basic knowledge of the process and the variables of patenting.

Chapter 4, "Ownership", takes a step backwards to identify the personal, legal and corporate issues around the ownership of patents, particularly those made by employees, whether or not related to their work.

Trademarks, design rights and other non-patent intellectual property rights are highlighted in Chapter 5. While most chapters address themselves mainly to readers interested in technical innovation, this book's focus on the economic perspective of protection requires the complementary treatise of these "soft" non-technical rights in this context. This protection, which is often more effective in the market and easier to enforce in court, is not of the inner technical "idea" or inventive essence of a product, but of its name and design. Capturing value through product innovation requires the protection of both marketing and technical elements.

Chapter 6, "Licensing", takes a corporate perspective, discussing the licensing of technology IP, exposing the reader to the complexity of commercial and competition law. In doing so, the reader will be prepared to address the key aspects of license drafting and to work fully and successfully with professional advisors.

Chapter 7, "Starting Up", revisits ideas around risk and return, and relates these carefully to the inventor or entrepreneur, outlining how to establish a start-up company around an intellectual property portfolio. Assuming that the inventor takes the advice of the previous chapters, Chapter 8 discusses the real-life application of tax laws around IP for both the individual and corporation. As becomes apparent, consideration of these parameters may have a profound influence on the overall financial balance of the inventive process.

"Intellectual Property Management" covers the spectrum of the patent world, from basic patenting to corporate taxation. This breadth is somewhat unusual, but reflects the authors' conviction that the effective and competitive management of innovation is dependent on an integrated and considered strategy. Engineers and scientists today must be encouraged to think about the commercial applicability and, more specifically, patentability of their inventions. Only with the careful definition of the economic drivers behind an invention, will such patenting create value for its inventors, and more widely, make a meaningful contribution to the broader economy. Poorly written and badly planned applications congest the legal and patent systems, lead to poor resource allocation and are an impediment to economic and technical development.

Well-written, granted patents, on the other hand, that respond to the commercial profile of the applicant, that can be licensed, and which are optimally adapted to the competitive landscape, will have fulfilled their potential, and that of the invention. That is the goal of this book.

Adam Levy and Claas Junghans
October 2005

Authors

Claas Junghans studied chemistry, molecular biology and intellectual property law in Berlin and has held senior management positions in several biotechnology companies.

Adam Levy has a Natural Sciences degree from Cambridge University and an MBA from INSEAD, Paris, and has held senior management and board positions in several start-up biotechnology companies.

Rolf Sander studied chemistry and physics, and practices intellectual property law as an in-house counsel for Siemens AG, and as German and European patent attorney at Stapel Rechtsanwälte, Berlin.

Tobias Boeckh studied chemistry and biochemistry in Berlin and practices patent law, trademark and design protection as a partner at Hertin, a law firm based in Berlin.

Jan Dirk Heerma is a partner in the Berlin office of the pan-european law firm SJ Berwin. He is head of SJ Berwin's Technology Group in Germany and specialises on licensing and R&D agreements and the IP-aspects of corporate transactions.

Christoph Regierer is a tax-lawyer and chartered auditor and practices corporate and tax law as a senior partner of Röver & Partner in Berlin. He is chairman of the European Fiscal and Tax Group of Moores Rowland International.

Intellectual Property Management. Claas Junghans, Adam Levy
Copyright © 2006 WILEY-VCH Verlag GmbH & Co. KGaA, Weinheim

Abbreviations

CTM	Community Trademark
ECLA	European Classification System
EP	European Patent, country code for the EPO
EPC	European Patent Convention
EPO	European Patent Office
IP	Intellectual Property
IPC	International Patent Classification
IR	International Registration
PCT	Patent Cooperation Treaty
USPTO	United States Patent Office
WIPO	World Intellectual Property Organization

Intellectual Property Management. Claas Junghans, Adam Levy
Copyright © 2006 WILEY-VCH Verlag GmbH & Co. KGaA, Weinheim

1
Terminology

Claas Junghans

For those who have had little or no prior exposure to the field, this chapter serves as a primer to the world of inventions and patents and introduces the topics that will be discussed in more depth in further chapters.

1.1
The Terms of Patenting

1.1.1
The Patent

Territoriality

A patent is a legal document that specifies a technical invention. Patents are territorial and relate to a specific country and the same invention can therefore be patented in a number of countries. Usually, these patents have the same owner, and are related to one another by their process of application; if that is the case, they form a patent family.

It is possible, however, for different owners to have rights to the same invention in different countries. This situation can arise if different applicants apply for patents on the same or similar inventions in different countries, or if the original inventor or applicant sells the patent rights for each country individually.

Exclusionary Rights

The owner of the patent is given certain rights to exclude others from making commercial use of an invention; specifically the right to exclude others from commercially using, selling, offering and keeping in stock an invention as specified in the claim section of the granted patent, in the particular country of the patent. Since the law governing patent protection differs across geographical jurisdictions, the scope of this protection varies for patents within the same family.

Similar exclusionary rights can be obtained on designs, and in certain cases on names used in the context of a business, termed trademarks. There are important differences between the protection of patents on technical inventions, also termed "utility patents", which are the main subject of this book, and design patents and trademarks, which are discussed in Chapter 5. Utility patents have a maximum term of 20 years from the day of filing the application; other forms of intellectual property (IP) have different terms.

Reward for Disclosure

The patentee is awarded the right to exclude competitors as a reward for the public disclosure of an innovation, intended to stimulate scientific development. To meet this criterion, however the patent must describe the invention in a way that enables others to reproduce the invention. US law is especially stringent in its demand for a "best mode" disclosure, non-fulfilment of which may lead to invalidation of the patent.

First-to-Apply

More than one inventor may independently make an invention. Europe and most other nations, with the exception of the USA, grant the patent right to the applicant who first files an application on the invention in their country. In the USA, the right to patent is granted to whomever first made the invention regardless of the time of filing. Efforts are ongoing to bring US law in line with the rest of the world, but it is not clear whether this particular harmonisation will be successful.

1.1.2
The Process of Patenting

Drafting

Patenting an invention is a formal process resembling a dialogue between the applicant, who submits a patent application on an invention, and the national or regional Patent Office, which decides whether and to what extent the invention is patentable.

The process of drafting entails the collection of all material describing the invention, as well as publications that describe the technical background of the invention. A skilled professional, most likely a patent attorney or in-house patent agent, then drafts a patent application specifying the invention in all necessary detail, and claiming the essential principle and important embodiments that are to be protected.

Application

The first formal step in achieving patent protection is the submission of a patent application. This application alone confers only marginal protection to its owner, and most countries grant provisional protection rights to the applicant after the application is made public, usually after 18 months.

An applicant may choose to send several patent applications originating from the same invention to different individual countries. Alternatively, an application can be submitted to trans-national offices acting on behalf of countries bound together by an international treaty. Examples of such transnational offices are the European Patent Office (EPO) and the office of the World Intellectual Property Organisation (WIPO). In most cases these pathways only facilitate the patenting process, and the applicant ultimately ends up with a family of national patents.

A "world patent" does not exist, but an application under the Patent Cooperation Treaty (PCT) allows the applicant to submit applications to a very large number of countries in a single filing. The applicant will send a "PCT filing" to a national or regional office, either as a first or as a follow-up filing. The applicant will then have up to 30 months after the initial first filing to decide in which other countries of the PCT member states an application should be submitted. Commercially, the most notable exception to PCT membership is Taiwan, which has instead bilateral treaties with most countries to the same effect.

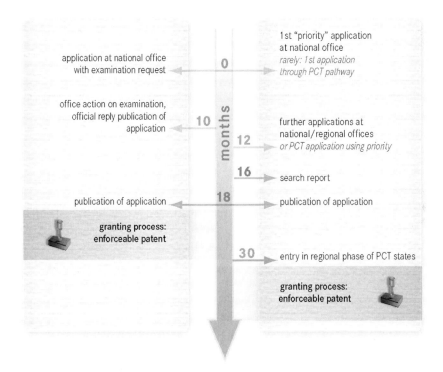

Fig. 1.1 Patent process: The national (left side) and the PCT pathway (right side) differ in how quickly an enforceable patent is issued. Many applicants choose the PCT pathway to file in many countries with one single application, because costs are deferred until later in the process.

Priority

Priority is a technical term referring to a ranking or "time-stamping" of inventions by calendar date. The earlier an invention has first been registered as a patent application at a Patent Office, the earlier its "priority". Of two applications that describe a similar invention, only the application with the earlier priority can give rise to a patent in any particular country.

A priority application can also be used as the basis for a second, extended application that encompasses its content. The content is then treated as if it had been submitted at the earlier priority date. The submission of an application therefore confers the right to be considered prior to others, and this right may extend to other applications.

This concept of a "priority right" was initially applied to individual offices, but today, most offices work together under the terms of an international treaty, the Paris Convention, in recognizing applications from other offices and priority rights can be used almost worldwide. The applicant may submit an application for a patent in only one country, and wait up to twelve months until submitting further applications relating to the same invention in many more countries. These later applications benefit from their claim to priority of the first application.

A follow-on application is granted a 20-year term, and an important result of submitting such applications using the priority of an initial filing is the effective prolongation of the invention's protection to 21 years. Whilst in fast-moving technologies this may have little importance, in technologies with long lifetimes, this mechanism may be very relevant to the total balance sheet of the patent.

Prior Art

Publications made before the priority date, which describe the elements and technology of the invention, form the "Prior Art". Publication does not have to be made in writing; public disclosure in a speech, or presentation, or over the internet also can form part of the prior art, though written disclosures are easier to track and date.

The existence of prior art describing an invention or elements of an invention, is an important weapon in contesting a patent, and a lot of prior art case law has therefore been compiled. Selling an invention before submitting a patent application, for instance, will in most cases make the invention part of the prior art, and hence unpatentable, even if the invention was not readily seen from the sold object. As always, however, what constitutes publication and what exact effect this has on patentability, is regulated nationally and may differ between countries.

Search Report

Many patent offices conduct a search of previous patent applications to identify the extent to which the claimed invention has been anticipated in the state of the art, or indeed, which documents can be found to come closest to the invention. The applicant thus receives official notification by a competent patent office as to which publications, if any, may interfere with the patentability of the invention. Decisions as to how to proceed with research and patenting activities may be influenced by this report. This search report is usually published with the application 18 months after the priority date.

Examination

Depending on the country, patent applications may be subject to mandatory examination, or may remain at the application state until the applicant or another interested party requests examination. The USPTO (United States Patent and Trademark Office) examines applications automatically without a need for further request. In many other jurisdictions however, the request for examination is a separate step in the procedure and can be delayed until a search report by the respective patent office has been issued. This gives the applicant a chance to amend or abandon the application in light of the findings of the search report.

For applications being processed by the European Patent Office, requesting the examination is mandatory within the first two years after application. Although there is a requirement to explicitly request examination before the EPO, the application form already contains this official request. The applicant must remember to pay the examination fee however. In Japan examination is mandatory three years after application and the German office requires no mandatory examination for the first seven years after the initial application.

Despite numerous differences in practice, all national and transnational offices require that formal and material requirements are met and that fees are paid. The examiner eventually issues a communication on the patentability of the submitted claims, and a dialogue ensues that will either lead to a granted patent or the abandonment of the application. Usually, failure to adhere to formal obligations stipulated by law or the corresponding office, or failure to pay the necessary fees, results in an application being deemed abandoned or withdrawn, although recourse may be possible.

Granting, Opposition and Revocation

If the patent is provisionally granted, it will be published by the relevant office. In many jurisdictions there then follows a period during which interested parties, often competitors, may submit a notice of opposition to the patent. In the case of the EPO this period lasts nine months. Other jurisdictions have a shorter opposition period (three months for the German office), or do not provide for opposition at all. US patent law does not currently provide for an opposition procedure, though it seems likely that one will be adopted within the next few years.

Once the patent is granted and any opposition period has expired, the last recourse against a patent is the process of revocation by the national courts. Revocation procedures are rare. Revocation aside, a granted patent will be in force for the duration of the patent term; 20 years from the date of the application from which it originated, provided maintenance fees are paid. In most countries, the patent owner must pay such maintenance fees in order for the patent to remain in force, and these fees usually rise steeply towards the end of the 20-year term. This is intended as an economic incentive to allow old patents to expire, allowing technology to become publicly available.

1.1.3
The Value in a Patent

The financial value of a patent stretching over its twenty-year lifespan is discussed fully in Chapters 6 and 7.

In-House Use, Licence or Sale

The immediate benefit that a patent confers to its owner is the power to exclude others from the use of the invention specified by the patent claims. This monopolistic power gives the patent owner special power in its market, and permits the realisation of greater profits. Four different principle mechanisms exist to derive value from a patent:

- an improved market position for the patented invention marketed as a product or employed as a process, directly by the patent owner ("in-house use"),
- revenue from licence payments paid to the patent owner by a third party operating under the cover of the patent,
- direct sale of the patent, or
- blocking or "fencing-in" of competitors, without making use of the patented invention.

The process by which value may be extracted from a patent is not as straightforward as a simple economic monopoly model would suggest however. It is complicated by inter-patent dependence, patent enforceability and cost issues.

Dependence and Multi-Patent Products

Often more than one patented technology is present in a product. If these technologies belong to different parties, their presence influences the ability of each patent owner to capture value. Indeed, the competing interests of the patent owners will need to be resolved in order for the product to be marketed, and for any of the parties to capture value from their inventions.

Different technologies may be independent of each other, such as the wheels and the chain of a bicycle. Often, however, there is some technological hierarchy or dependence. One frequent example is a patented improvement of an already patented innovation.

Such dependence can effectively bar an inventor or patentee from using an invention. It cannot be sufficiently stressed that owning a patent is not a licence to practise the patented invention; the power conferred by the patent is purely to exclude others from the practice of that invention (see Box 1).

Box 1
Dependency

Consider the invention of the steam cooker. The principle of this invention is to cook food in hot, pressurized steam. The simplest essential equipment for practicing the invention could be a pot with a steam-sealed lid, and a patent on the invention would have an independent claim reading:

- Apparatus for the cooking of food comprising a pot (1) and a lid (2), characterized by the lid being fastened to the pot in a steam-tight fashion, creating a chamber (3) that can be pressurized.

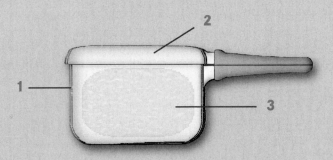

In the absence of a mechanism to avoid the formation of pressure above the technical limit of the pot's material, the steam cooker is likely to explode if not heated carefully. The need for technical improvement is clear.

If a second inventor came up with a safety valve, this invention would certainly aid the safety and marketability of the product. A claim on this invention may read:

- Steam cooking apparatus comprising a pot (1) and a lid (2), where the lid is fastened to the pot in a steam tight manner creating a steam-tight chamber (3), characterized by a safety valve (4) being comprised in one of the enclosures of the steam-tight chamber.

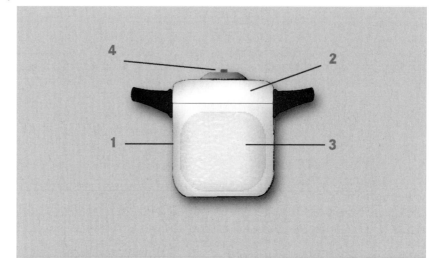

The owner of the initial patent could market the pot alone, without the safety valve, and is legally independent. The second inventor, however, could not market the pot-cum-valve without a licence from the owner of the initial patent, since this invention includes all the elements of the first claim. The second inventor is dependent on the first.

Economically, however, the first inventor cannot sell pots without a valve, since they tend to explode. This inventor is legally independent, but in the absence of a technical alternative to the safety valve, is economically dependent on the valve technology to make the steam cooker pots marketable. The first inventor is "fenced in". If it is in the commercial interests of the inventors, the twin issues of dependency and fencing-in can be addressed by patent cross-licensing.

Enforcement

The cost and practicality of patent enforcement is an important issue. The value of a patent is derived from the power it confers to engage in litigation against competitors who make commercial use of the patented invention without having obtained a licence. Such competitors must be identified, demonstrated to be in contravention of the patent, and compelled to make amends; overall, an expensive process.

The detection and demonstration of infringement requires a network of local surveillance. Large multinational companies have such systems in place, but smaller businesses operating from a single location must invest in this architecture. If the patent relates to a physical object, it is possible to substantiate infringement easily, but if the patent relates to a process, proof of infringement may be more difficult, particularly if the process relates to a product that can be made by a number of routes. Whilst proof may ultimately be attainable, this comes at a significant cost.

The subsequent process of enforcing a patent includes, in its extreme form, lengthy and expensive court battles involving specialist lawyers. The overall cost of this legal enforcement greatly depends on the case, and potential litigants must consider both the merits of their legal arguments and the likely response of the infringer. Some large companies have significant resources and a history of stringent and successful litigation. Confrontation will be regarded differently depending on the situation of the patentee; a university clerk bound to a strict budget, the owner of a small business, or a large multinational protecting a key patent will all have different attitudes to the risk and cost of litigation.

There is no recipe for patent enforcement; only a principle. Legal enforcement is an integral conclusion to the patent value chain, to be avoided if possible, but considered from the outset of application.

Costs

A balance must be struck between the expected value of a patent and the costs of securing and enforcing it. These costs can vary immensely. Important variables are the pathway the applicant chooses to pursue, in which countries the invention is to be patented, whether and which patent lawyers or agents are employed, the field and scope of the invention, and the amount of correspondence between the office and the patent agent.

A valid patent can be registered for under $500 in the US; similar figures for Germany and the UK are about €500 and £200, respectively. These figures include examination fees levied by the patent offices, but no legal fees paid to an attorney or representative. Substantial worldwide protection, managed by a patent agent or attorney and through the necessary network of local representatives, can cost significantly upward of 100.000 €. Indeed, even restricting oneself to the major markets in Europe, the Americas and Asia may carry a similar cost.

The delicate balance between cost and value is individual to each patent and each applicant. Not all costs arise immediately after filing, and nor must an invention reach the market before a return can be made. The sophisticated applicant is able to devise a strategy to maximise the return based on their level of investment, and on their appetite for risk. This relationship between cost, value and risk is a major topic of this book.

1.1.4
Anatomy of a Patent Document

Front Page

The Front Page of a patent application shows the title of the invention and the issuing organization or country and presents information pertaining to the type of document, the inventors and the applicants, references to documents in the same family, and most importantly, to key dates in the patenting schedule. Since the reader may not be familiar with the language or even the script of a document, a code has been established that associates datasets with numbers. For example,

PCT

WORLD INTELLECTUAL PROPERTY ORGANIZATION
International Bureau

INTERNATIONAL APPLICATION PUBLISHED UNDER THE PATENT COOPERATION TREATY (PCT)

(51) International Patent Classification 4 : A63H 3/20, 3/46	A1	(11) International Publication Number: WO 87/ 03502
		(43) International Publication Date: 18 June 1987 (18.06.87)

(21) International Application Number: PCT/DK86/00130

(22) International Filing Date: 3 December 1986 (03.12.86)

(31) Priority Application Number: 5608/85

(32) Priority Date: 4 December 1985 (04.12.85)

(33) Priority Country: DK

(71) Applicant *(for AU only):* INTERLEGO A.G. [CH/CH]; Sihlbruggstrasse 3, CH-6340 Baar (CH).

(71) Applicant *(for all designated States except AU US):* INTERLEGO A/S [DK/DK]; Aastvej 1, DK-7190 Billund (DK).

(72) Inventors; and
(75) Inventors/Applicants *(for US only)* : RYAA, Jan [DK/DK]; Kærvej 423, DK-7190 Billund (DK). POULSEN, Ole, Vestergaard [DK/DK]; Arne Pulsensvej 3, DK-7100 Vejle (DK).

(74) Agent: HOFMAN-BANG & BOUTARD A/S; Adelgade 15, DK-1304 Copenhagen K (DK).

(81) Designated States: AT (European patent), AU, BE (European patent), BG, BR, CH (European patent), DE (European patent), FI, FR (European patent), GB (European patent), HU, IT (European patent), JP, KR, LU (European patent), NL (European patent), NO, SE (European patent), SU, US.

Published
With international search report.

(54) Title: A TOY FIGURE HAVING MOVABLE BODY PARTS

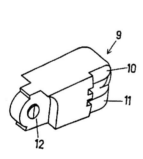

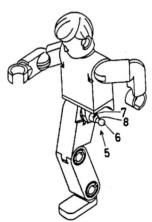

(57) Abstract

In a toy figure with body parts movable in various directions the body parts (in the embodiment shown the legs) are connected with the body in a manner known per se by means of a socket (13) designed to receive a ball (6). To ensure long-term frictional stability between the movable parts, the body part (9) is formed with a pair of opposed walls (10, 11) designed to squeeze an engagement face (7) which is contiguous with the ball (6).

Fig. 1.2 The front page of an international application under the Patent Cooperation Treaty (PCT). Reproduced with permission by WIPO and the European Patent Office/espacenet.

(22) codifies the filing date of an application, and (71) the applicant. These numbers may not be present on older applications.

The examining office also gives patents or applications unique identifying numbers, and these appear both in the patent database and on the front page of any patent document. These numbers provide information as to the type, geography and status of a patent application. Usually, both applications and granted patents appear in databases as a combination of letters indicating the country, followed by a number and a letter. The letter "A" denotes applications, and this is changed to a "B" upon grant of a patent. There may be subsequent numbers and letters other than A and B depending on the country. The exact codes used by every country and their significance can be found on patent office websites.

Description and Drawings

The main section of a patent document always specifies the invention in words, and often in drawings. Typically, the description begins with a summary of the field of the invention and the technical shortcomings of the state of the art. Reference is made to the technology upon which the invention improves. This general section is often concluded by the formulation of a particular technical problem posed by the state of the art.

The invention will then be described in general terms and in detailed examples. Often, statements will be included in the description that make sweeping claims about what embodiments and alternative solutions to the technical problem fall within "the scope of the invention". The description in many patents will be worded so as to be very far-reaching.

It is important for the novice in the field to realise that this description does not define the exclusionary rights conferred by the patent. It is rather the "claims" of a patent that act to define these exclusionary rights. The description supports the claims, and in cases of doubt, offices and judges will refer to the content of the description in determining the exact scope of the claims.

Claims

The claims of an application define the exclusionary rights that the applicant wants to reserve, though these are often subsequently narrowed by examiners to meet patentability criteria. A claim is a one-sentence definition of the invention (technically not even a proper sentence, as the main verb is missing), but since inventions may be complicated, a claim can be very long and complex in wording. One way to analyse this complexity is to break the claim down into components or elements. An element is the indivisible base unit of the invention.

To infringe or fall under the scope of a claim, any product or process must comprise or contain all the elements of the claim. Claims, therefore, with few elements cover a wide area of technology, as products are more likely to comprise all the elements of such claims. Such claims are said to be broad. Broad claims suffer from a higher likelihood of the existence of prior art, and are more likely to be

INTERNATIONAL SEARCH REPORT

International Application No PCT/DK86/00130

I. CLASSIFICATION OF SUBJECT MATTER (if several classification symbols apply, indicate all) *

According to International Patent Classification (IPC) or to both National Classification and IPC ₄

A 63 H 3/20, A 63 H 3/46

II. FIELDS SEARCHED

Minimum Documentation Searched ⁷

Classification System	Classification Symbols
IPC	A 63 H 3/16, /20, /46
Nat Cl	77f: 3/16, /20, /46
US Cl	46: 161, 163

Documentation Searched other than Minimum Documentation
to the Extent that such Documents are Included in the Fields Searched ⁸

SE, NO, DK, FI classes as above

III. DOCUMENTS CONSIDERED TO BE RELEVANT ⁹

Category *	Citation of Document, ¹¹ with Indication, where appropriate, of the relevant passages ¹²	Relevant to Claim No. ¹³
A	SE, A, 83 065 (DEICHMANN) 2 April 1935	1-4
A	DK, C, 69 266 (MÄTSEPURO) 23 May 1949	1-4
A	FR, A, 1 386 510 (RIBOUD) 22 January 1965	1-4
A	US, A, 1 868 049 (DEICHMANN) 19 July 1932	1-4

* Special categories of cited documents: ¹⁰
"A" document defining the general state of the art which is not considered to be of particular relevance
"E" earlier document but published on or after the International filing date
"L" document which may throw doubts on priority claim(s) or which is cited to establish the publication date of another citation or other special reason (as specified)
"O" document referring to an oral disclosure, use, exhibition or other means
"P" document published prior to the international filing date but later than the priority date claimed

"T" later document published after the international filing date or priority date and not in conflict with the application but cited to understand the principle or theory underlying the invention
"X" document of particular relevance; the claimed invention cannot be considered novel or cannot be considered to involve an inventive step
"Y" document of particular relevance; the claimed invention cannot be considered to involve an inventive step when the document is combined with one or more other such documents, such combination being obvious to a person skilled in the art.
"&" document member of the same patent family

IV. CERTIFICATION

Date of the Actual Completion of the International Search	Date of Mailing of this International Search Report
1987-03-06	1987-03-10

International Searching Authority	Signature of Authorized Officer
Swedish Patent Office	Manfred Weiss

Form PCT/ISA/210 (second sheet) (January 1985)

Fig. 1.3 The international search report of the application shown on the previous page. All cited prior art is labelled "A": the office considered the documents found in the search of no particular relevance with regard to the patentability of the patent's claims. Such report is a good indication that the claims have a high probability to be granted in examination. (Reproduced with permission by WIPO and the European Patent Office/espacenet.)

found non-patentable by examiners. In addition to broad, independent claims, patent agents therefore usually draft "dependent" claims with additional elements to provide a fallback.

If a product does not contain all elements of the claim, it does not fall under the scope of the claim. If it contains all elements of the claim, and at least one more, it falls under the scope of the claim and yet may constitute a novel invention (see Box 1).

The Research Report Page

Patents and applications that have been submitted to a formal search of relevant literature by a patent office contain a section with the citations of identified prior art. This information can be a valuable indicator of what prior art has been considered in the granting of the patent, or what prior art the office may consider in a subsequent examination.

The search report format chosen by the European Patent Office (EP documents ending in A1 or A3) and similarly used in documents published by the PCT pathway (document numbers beginning with WO) is especially useful. Possibly relevant documents are given with an indicator of their importance to the patentability of the claims. Prior art labelled as X or Y renders the patentability of a claim at least dubious. The report is useful in giving a competitor or potential investor a formal opinion on the patentability of the claimed invention.

1.1.5
Patentability of an Invention

Invention

Although the colloquial term "invention" means many things to many people, the law of each country has clear definitions of what constitutes a patentable invention. For the purpose of patent law, an invention is a new solution to a technical problem, which meets stringent criteria of novelty, inventiveness and technical content. These legal criteria may vary, in some cases enormously, from one country to the next. Although a process of harmonisation is currently under way it will be several years until these differences in patentability criteria become extinct.

Product, Process and Method Claims

An invention can be manifest in a physical object – a machine or a part of a machine or a chemical compound. Alternatively, it can be evident in a way of acting or doing things, as a process or a method of using a certain set of physical objects. Hence, patents can contain both claims to a product and an activity.

Sometimes a certain object, often a chemical compound, may be easiest to claim not by definitions applicable to the object itself, but to the process of making the object or compound. While such claims have an activity in their defining language, they refer to a product. Patents will often have claims to both products and actions so as to optimally protect all manifestations of an inventive idea.

Novelty

One absolute criterion for patentability is novelty: the claimed invention must not have been known before the day of application or indeed, the priority date, if a priority is claimed. If all the elements of a claim can be found in one "embodiment" (a single object or process) known in the state of the art preceding the date of first application, that claim will not be patentable. The novelty of a claim is not destroyed, however, if its elements are anticipated in different embodiments.

US law does not refer to the day of application to define novelty, but rather to the day of invention. Thus, an invention inadvertently published prior to submitting a patent application may still be patentable in the US, but nowhere else in the world. A special case arises when no published prior art existed on the day of application of a patent, but a similar invention had already been submitted, awaiting publication. Such "prior rights" will preclude patentability only in the countries where the prior rights were filed.

Non-Obviousness

Not only must a claimed invention not have been anticipated by the state of the art, it must also be sufficiently different from its closest relative in the state of the art. In patent terms, it must differ to such a degree that it required an "inventive step" to come up with the invention. This principle prevents anyone from combining known elements from the state of the art into a novel object or process and claiming this obvious combination as a patent.

Despite this seemingly fuzzy definition, the practice of patent law has come up with pragmatic ways of deciding whether any particular claim meets the inventive step criteria. The subject of non-obviousness is discussed more fully in Chapter 3.

Non-Disclosure

The requirements of novelty and non-obviousness are absolute. If the invention has been made public knowledge before the application, even by the applicant or inventor, the invention is considered to be part of the state of the art, and hence, not patentable. In the US, a so-called "grace period" exists, but it would be highly recommendable even for US inventors not to publish their inventions lest they destroy their chances of being granted a patent in the rest of the world.

This principle of non-disclosure prior to registering an application does not mean that inventors cannot discuss their invention, and indeed such discussions with patent agents and investors are necessary. Inventors must simply take proper precautions to ensure that the invention is not made available to the public. Certain relationships, such as the attorney-client relationship or a working relationship between co-operating companies will imply an obligation to secrecy. It is very advisable, however, to take any precaution possible to exclude preliminary publication of an invention. Standard non-disclosure agreements ensure adherence to this principle.

Patentable Matter

Utility patents can only protect technical inventions. Inventions relating to the aesthetic qualities of an object, such as its shape or colour, without solving a technical problem, can be protected by design patents. Software and business methods are deemed non-technical and are thus excluded from patentability in many patent systems of the world, including Europe. The US Patent and Trademark Office (USPTO) accepts such applications and regularly grants patents on inventions that would be deemed non-technical under current standards at the EPO. Similarly, procedures to treat the human or animal body are not patentable in Europe, though devices used for such procedures are patentable.

1.1.6
Inventors and Applicants

All patent systems recognize the inventor as the original owner of an idea. The right to the patent, however, resides with the applicant.

Inventorship

The authors of an invention must be named on a patent application. They are the original owners of the right to the invention, although they may be in contractual obligation to cede this right.

One key activity at the outset of the patenting process is to identify the inventors. This may be difficult and sometimes cause conflict, but it is a very important decision. The exclusion of inventors from the patent may damage working relations, and jeopardize the legal validity and economic value of the patent. On the other hand, a large group of inventors may be difficult to manage.

The identity of the inventors is dependent on the invention that is claimed, under patentability criteria. This is influenced by the "prior art" found in the drafting process. Proper process should be observed and an attorney should be consulted, particularly if the invention is to be patented in the USA. Generally the criteria for inventorship are more stringent than those usually applied to the authorship of scientific publications. Inventors must have contributed to solving the underlying problem in a way that was not routine or obvious.

The Inventor as Applicant

Patent offices make the distinction between the inventor and the applicant, who is the person or entity with whom the Patent Office deals. If the applicant is not the inventor, some justification as to how the applicant gained the right to apply is formally requested.

Indeed, in the US, only the inventors have the right to apply for a patent. The role of the corporate or university entity that has sponsored the invention is that of assignee. The assignee is named on the application or patent, but formally, the inventor has the role of the applicant, and hence, primary ownership of the patent, to which the assignee may be a successor in title.

Since most R&D work today is performed by corporate or academic entities and pursuing the patenting of an invention in multiple countries can be a costly venture, the inventor-applicant model is not as common outside of the US as it may once have been.

The Applicant as Successor in Title

Outside the US, this configuration is the most common. Corporate or academic sponsors of research will often oblige their employees to yield any inventions to the employer. Some countries stipulate this succession by law.

Several issues arise when looking in detail at this employer-inventor situation, and these are discussed in detail in Chapter 4. In effect, the relationship between employer and inventor may resemble that of a licensee-licensor, with an over-riding and potentially conflicting employer-employee relationship. Large differences exist between countries in the approach to resolving this inherent conflict. Another issue may arise if the inventor is in a contractual relationship with more than one party. This may arise when two full-time employments fall in quick succession and the origin of the invention is difficult to allocate, or when the inventor has effectively worked for more than one party at the same time.

1.2
Business Brief

Patents are exclusionary rights and do not imply any right or licence of the owner to use or sell the patented invention. The issued patent is a "right to sue" upon infringement.

Patents are territorial and an invention enjoys protection only in the countries in which patents have been applied for and have been issued. Not all types of inventions are patentable in all countries.

Applications and issued patents must be distinguished. Applications only confer provisional and limited protection. A patent application on an invention may take between one and more than four years to become a patent. If the examining office does not agree that the invention is patentable, a patent may not be issued and no protection is attained. Indeed, references made to a "patented invention" may often mean only that an application has been submitted. Resulting patent protection may be conditional on further examination.

After a patent is granted, many countries allow the public to oppose the patent for a limited period. Patents may later be attacked only by initiating a revocation process.

Care must be taken to keep an invention unpublished prior to filing an application in at least one of the Patent Cooperation Treaty member countries, to which most commercially important countries belong. Publication will render the invention unpatentable. Inventors must use non-disclosure agreements when discussing the invention with business partners and refrain from selling or using the invention publicly prior to application.

Patented technology may be dependent on other patents, thus forcing anyone making use of such technology to obtain a licence for the umbrella patents that dominate. Patents or indeed, entire portfolios may block each other.

Minimal information such as patent numbers enables a patent attorney to form a preliminary opinion about the validity of a patent family. In order to give an opinion about the value of a portfolio however, much more information is needed, including an assessment of the competition and of the technical field.

The applicant must have a valid claim to the ownership of the invention, and due diligence should be taken in ascertaining the validity of ownership transfer.

Value may be derived from a patent through use, licence or sale, or by blocking competitors. The anticipated value must be balanced by the costs of patenting and enforcement.

2
The Economic Objectives of Protection

Claas Junghans

The purpose of this chapter is to enable the reader to clearly position patents within the context of business strategy. Whilst patents are technical in substance and legal in structure, their pursuit requires the consumption of both human and financial resources, and the decision to allocate these resources is a rational economic one.

Before delving more deeply into the technical and legal elements of patenting, the reader is therefore advised to invest considerable thought in the overall business purpose of patenting. It is likely, and highly advised, that the reader will employ a patent attorney to both draft applications and provide counsel on patent strategy. The attorney's ability to translate business needs into a patent portfolio is dependent on the applicants communication of clearly defined economic objectives. In the absence of these goals, even the most qualified and diligent of patent attorneys will make assumptions about the applicants needs. The results are at best unnecessary costs, and at worst, bad patents that do not match the economic drivers of the application.

The generation of intellectual property is a complex endeavour, requiring investment of both time and money. Much can be done to optimize the yield of this investment if clear objectives are stated early in the process, and a plan is made to attain these objectives. Many resources are poorly spent because such commonplace advice is not followed. Applicants will be in a variety of situations with regards to their industry, technology, financial circumstance and competitive environment. Hence, the detailed objectives in patenting discussed here, will be different for each inventor or applicant. Nevertheless, standard elements of situations can be identified and a combination of these elements will, to some degree, resemble the scenario in which readers find themselves.

This chapter studies two key fundamental elements of patent strategy; the route of filing, and the breadth of claims. It discusses each element and considers the factors that drive value generation for each.

Intellectual Property Management. Claas Junghans, Adam Levy
Copyright © 2006 WILEY-VCH Verlag GmbH & Co. KGaA, Weinheim

2.1
Filing Strategy

The applicant must determine the timing of application and the number, and sequence of countries in which an invention will be registered as a patent.

2.1.1
When to File?

The simple answer as to when to file the first application is: as early as possible after having obtained substantial proof of an invention. The greatest risk for any applicant is that of being pre-empted by a competitor filing a similar or closely related invention. A competing invention submitted earlier may render the applicant's claims unpatentable and may ultimately mean that the applicant is subject to exclusion by the competing patent.

Chapter 3 discusses the criteria for the sufficient disclosure of material. It is important that the application discloses not only an idea but a workable technical solution to a real problem. If this criterion is not satisfied, the patent may not be issued, or, if approved, may be liable to attack by competitors. US law has especially stringent requirements as to sufficient disclosure. This is important when filing in the US through the USPTO, or indeed if any application filed outside the US is to be used for claiming priority before the USPTO.

2.1.2
Where to File: National Offices and International Treaties

To the unitiated there appears an intimidating myriad of routes to achieving patent protection. Fundamentally, the process is a national one; application in a territory is followed by local examination and, if all goes well, the grant of a patent, which is locally enforceable. To reduce the inefficiencies of multiple patent applications however, there exist a number of international treaties that define how countries can work in concert to consider, grant and enforce patent applications. These treaties are identified in Box 2. As discussed below, however, these create a range of options for the applicant.

Box 2
International Patent Treaties

(for lists of member states, see Annex 1–3)

The **Paris Convention**, to which a great many countries are signatories, grants the right to use the priority date of an application in any member country in all the other countries of the treaty.

The **Patent Cooperation Treaty (PCT)** regulates a unified application pathway to allow applicants simultaneously, and with a single application, to apply for a patent in several countries. Patents are not issued by the PCT pathway, but by the individual member states or regional offices named as designated states in the PCT application form. A preliminary examination can be requested in the PCT pathway.

The **European Patent Convention** (EPC) is an agreement between its member states to unify the patent application and granting process within Europe. The applicant submits a patent application to the **European Patent Office**, which processes and, if the result of the examination is positive, issues a European Patent. The European Patent then must be registered with the national offices to become valid in each specific country. All countries of the European union are members of the EPC, but also many non-EU members, such as Switzerland and Turkey. The EPO performs a similar function to a national office. The cost, however of filing through the EPO, is lower than simultaneously filing in several EPC member states.

Other regional treaties, the Eurasian Patent Organisation EAPO, the OAPI and the ARIPO, regulate applications in Eurasia, and the French- and English-speaking African countries respectively.

National Pathways

Patents are granted and enforced at a national level, and different offices have a different approach to allowing certain claims. The result of an examination may differ particularly between US and European offices.

The quickest patent application pathway therefore is to file directly and immediately in the desired territories. Each office will then examine each patent according to national regulations. Much of the cost of patenting is incurred early, including office and translation fees. If the invention is found to be patentable however, this is the fastest route to the grant of enforceable exclusionary power.

European Pathway

A European Patent is essentially a single application process covering a bundle of national filings. The application is submitted to the European Patent Office, which performs a review of the prior art and examines the application, on behalf of its constituent territories. If the examiner agrees to the patentability of the submitted claims, a European Patent is issued. More details of this process are given in the next chapter.

Fees have to be paid at different stages of the process and the total office fees from application to grant are in the range of 4000 Euro[1].

Once the European Patent is issued it is automatically valid in all designated states and the application is not re-examined by the offices of each country. The applicant must pay for translation into the national languages of the countries in which it is to be effective, and national fees must be paid. Translation is expensive relative to the EPO fees and annual maintenance fees must be paid to the national offices.

A European Patent Application can be submitted as a first application without priority, as a secondary application claiming the priority of another national, European or PCT application, or the European Office can be elected in a PCT application. In this latter case, the EPO procedure is delayed until the national phase of the PCT pathway.

PCT Pathway

In the PCT pathway one application is submitted to a single Patent Office acting on behalf of the World International Property Organisation (WIPO), or the WIPO central office itself. This office processes the application according to the PCT treaty provisions. For every application, a search report is published 18 months after the priority date of the invention. A preliminary examination can be sought by applying to have the International Application examined by the competent office. The examination can be ordered at any time during this first phase of the PCT process.

However at no stage does the PCT application become a valid patent, conferring exclusionary rights. This quality is only achieved after the national phase, which may be entered into up to 30 months after the initial priority filing. Then, the applicant has to send copies of the PCT application, along with a translation to the corresponding national language, to the national offices. This national phase can be very expensive, depending on the number of countries and the size of the application.

The strategic function of the PCT pathway is that of a "waiting room". It gives the applicant an additional 18 months of time on top of the 12 months accorded by the right to priority under the Paris Convention, to decide where and how to pursue the protection of the invention. Any resultant patent is not enforceable until completion of the national phase after this time.

If possible, an early decision should be made as to the extent of territorial protection which will be ultimately required, and whether the corresponding applications will be filed immediately and directly, or through the PCT mechanism, with or without the use of the priority period.

Filing one national application first and using the priority of this application to file a PCT application before the expiry of the 12-month priority period expires is a standard way. This method combines low initial costs with the options to decide the territorial extent of the protection after 30 months.

[1] Office fees may vary depending on the size of the application, the number of claims, the number of designated states for which the application is to be applied. All fees are given as an approximate value at the end of the year 2004.

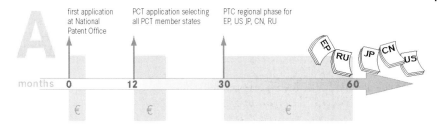

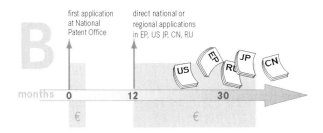

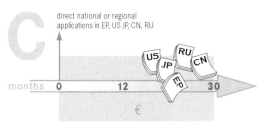

Fig. 2.1 Possible alternative filing strategies. **A**: The invention is deposited with a national office. Within 12 months, a PCT filing is deposited. Costs for both applications are moderate (grey boxes). Costs are incurred again at the end of the 30 month-deadline of the PCT international period, when the application must be regionalized (here: before the EPO, in the USA, Japan, China and Russia), translated into the respective languages and submitted through local attorneys. The issueance of patents depends on many factors and can take up to five years. **B**: A national application is filed to determine a priority date for the invention; within 12 months, national applications are filed directly. Costs are incurred earlier, but patents are issued more quickly. **C**: the invention is protected by simultaneous applications in national and regional offices. This strategy, paired with accelerated publication and examination, is very high-risk but leads to the accelerated generation of enforceable rights if the invention is found patentable.

2.1.3
Where to First File?

The applicant must determine to which patent agency the initial application is to be made. This first step is important in that it defines much of what follows. Whilst follow-on filings confer additional territorial protection, first filing determines the speed and cost distribution of the application process.

Essentially, the choice to be made is whether to file the majority of national applications rather late, delaying the costs of translations and national attorneys' fees until shortly before the end of the 30-month-deadline, or whether to incur the costs of national applications relatively early, with a correspondingly accelerated patent grant and enforceable exclusionary rights.

Accelerated Examination

Some patent offices offer an accelerated examination process within the first 12 months following an application. This allows the applicant to determine whether the application will succeed and whether it is therefore worth pursuing in many countries. Among others, the British, European and the German offices offer such service, and a similar mechanism exists in the US. The availability of this option may be dependent on office workload, and an attorney should be consulted to assure that all necessary requirements for accelerated examination are met. Accelerated examination is a cost-effective means to receive a formal opinion if doubt exists as to the patentability of the invention or whether specific claims are allowable.

2.1.4
Follow-up Filings and the Territorial Extent of Protection

Filing through the PCT mechanism delays filing in national territories by a maximum of 18 months, from 12 months after the initial priority-defining application; it does not replace this local filing. The additional fees in office costs for PCT filing are in the range of 5000 € including a preliminary examination. This preliminary examination reduces some of the later costs in certain countries. The additional legal costs for preparation of the PCT application will be dependent on circumstances such as the type of invention, the volume of the supporting description and the attorney.

The net extra cost of the PCT procedure is small therefore in comparison to the total cost of a comprehensive patenting approach in many countries. The delay in the decision on where to file provides the opportunity to reduce the risk of investing in a bundle of applications that may not be granted. If the invention is to be protected in more than a small handful of countries, the additional cost of the PCT application is therefore offset by the reduction in overall risk. Nevertheless, it is important to again point out that the PCT pathway not only delays the decision where to file, but also the eventual issue of patents. If protection is needed early in fast-moving markets, applying directly, or combining national and PCT pathways, may be an alternative strategy.

2.2
Claim Breadth: The Scope of the Desired Protection

Aside from filing strategy, the extent of the technological area covered by the claims is the other variable under immediate control of the applicant. This claim breadth has a significant influence on the economic value of the patent.

The general tendency of the applicant and the attorney will be to file as broad claims as possible. If granted, these provide optimal protection against competing technology, yielding wide exclusionary power in the market, and strengthening negotiations to license or sell the patent.

As a rule however, the examining office will be more likely to find prior art relating to broad claims, and whilst outright challenges of novelty may be avoided by rigorous searching, the discussion of inventive step in the examination process may become significantly more challenging if much prior art close to the broad claim exists. This prior art may form the grounds of fundamental uncertainty as to the patentability of any claim. The increased likelihood of this challenge raises the risk of prolonged procedures, higher costs for the increased attorney work, and legal challenges of the patent by competitors. The groundwork necessary to substantiate broader claims may further necessitate an increased level of research.

2.3
Factors Influencing Filing Strategy and Claim Breadth

2.3.1
The Invention, the Product and its Market

The Life-Cycle and Time-to-Market Period
The maximum term of a patent is 20 years from the day of filing, and it may take between two and more than five years for a patent to be issued, depending on the issuing office and a number of factors intrinsic to the invention. In formulating patent strategy these timescales need to be considered in light of the life-cycle and time-to-market of the invention.

Some areas of technology are characterised by a very rapid technological turnover, with innovations being pushed onto the market within months of invention and rendered obsolete in rapid succession, and entire markets being cannibalised within few years by newer technologies. Consumer electronics may be one such example. On the other end of the time scale, the pharmaceutical industry typically needs more than 10 years to bring a new chemical entity to the market, and some of its products are immensely lucrative up to, and beyond, patent expiry.

Patent strategy needs to adapt to such different time scales. Only an examined and granted patent confers serious exclusionary power to its owner. Inventions with short time-to-market periods require strategies that lead to swiftly granted patents. Furthermore, the closer an innovation is to the market at the time of first filing, the better the applicant's ability to gauge in which countries the invention needs protection. This renders "waiting rooms" such as the PCT pathway less of a necessity.

If the life-cycle of an invention is short because it is likely to be rapidly superseded by newer innovations, protracted and expensive filing procedures are not attractive, and the swiftest way to achieve multi-national protection is to apply directly to the various national offices, in the extreme form even forgoing the one-year priority period. Furthermore, there are limited, if any, advantages in extending the effective term of protection to 21 years by filing a follow-up application after 12 months under priority.

An invention that carries a high initial risk of failure, as is the case in pharmaceutical research, benefits from a strategy that delays the decision to commit significant resources to the patenting process. Hence, for "slow" technologies, the PCT filing strategy will be attractive. This allows the applicant to wait two and a half years before committing to applications in individual countries. This maintains an applicants options over most territories for a relatively modest additional fee (under € 5000 plus attorney fees). Similarly, inventions with a prospective market lifetime of over 20 years will benefit from the extra year of protection that is conferred when filing an additional application under priority. The patent arising from the additional application under patent will have its own term of twenty years, beginning one year after the initial filing and thus extending the total lifetime of protection to 21 years.

2.3.2
Market Economics

Patenting decisions must ultimately be made country by country and careful consideration needs to be given both to the profitability of any given territory, and the strategic importance of territories.

Geographic Difference in Investment Return

When considering the geographic scope of a patent, the applicant will balance the costs of patenting against the benefit of achieving exclusionary rights in each territory. The cost of filing and pursuing a patent application can differ dramatically for different countries, especially when translations and attorney costs are added to the fees levied by the respective patent office. Even when filing in the countries of the European Patent Convention, the costs of entering the national phase can differ greatly. National regulations differ in their requirement for the applicant to be represented by a national representative, and translation costs also differ significantly between languages.

If a product can generate large profits however, in any given market, even very high local patenting costs are a valuable investment. Pharmaceutical products, which can command very high margins when enjoying single-product status in a market, are one example where high costs of patenting become trivial in comparison to the opportunities offered even by small markets.

Despite good rationale for broad investment in patents, small companies are often faced with the question of the allocation of a limited IP budget. When the national fees discussed above are considered against the size and economic weight of a given country it is evident that some countries are very much more profitable than others (see the example in Box 3).

Box 3
To Patent in the USA or Portugal?

To take an example, in extremis, imagine a hypothetical small American company deciding whether to patent its invention across the Atlantic in Portugal.

- Cost of US patent to US company, with in-house patent officer,
  no attorney – $ 500
- Cost of PCT or EP extension to Portugal – $ 5000 (local fees,
  translation)
- GDP of USA – $ 11 trillion
- GDP of Portugal – $ 150 million

Considering the GDP as an approximate measure of the market potential for a product on a GDP weighted basis it is 700,000 times more expensive to patent in Portugal than in the USA. Indeed, one may find that apart from initial convenience, even a Portuguese firm may have little incentive to protect in its own country if the IP budget is tight and there is little or no immediate local competition.

Economies of Scale

Many industries benefit from a significant reduction in manufacturing costs when large volumes are produced. A company that has exclusivity in a few large markets through patenting in these markets, may therefore be able to reduce the costs of a product to such an extent that it is able to dominate markets in which no patent protects the product. If patents cover the main markets of Europe, the US and Asia, a competitor forced to operate at lower volume may find its products prohibitively expensive in the remaining markets.

Economies of scale alone do not permit monopolistic pricing in a country, and the extent to which this local barrier-to-entry can defend a market varies greatly from industry to industry. The decision to defend a market through economies of scale rather than patents is one that must be given considerable thought therefore.

Globally Traded Products

The strategies and behaviours of the companies to whom patent applicants intend to market their products must be taken into account when defining the territories of application, by reference to the return on investment of a specific territory.

For example, if the applicant can be certain that the invention will be part of a mass-produced, globally-traded product, such as a car or a television set, the patenting strategy may be able focus on key market territories. One patented component renders the overall product (the car or television set) susceptible to the legal effect of the patent. If a component were patented in, for example, the five main European markets, a competitor without patent would be able to sell the same component to be built into the car or TV only for the minor markets. A manufacturer, introducing competition into component sourcing, would only be able to distribute his product in these minor markets. This would compromise the overall manufacturing efficiency for a marginal cost reduction. The inventor through extrapolating the actions of the companies in its supply chain is therefore able to gain broad territorial control, whilst focussing its own strategy solely on major markets.

Emerging Markets

This consideration of revenue, scale and strategy, however, may drastically change over time as emerging markets evolve into potential generators of large volume sales and revenue, and as the legal and commercial structures within these economies develop, along with the capability to enforce patents. With some Asian and European countries experiencing rapid economic growth, the opportunities for a patent holder may significantly change over the 20-year term of a patent. China, for example, is now considered to be a more important territory than the US or Europe for some major industries.

The time horizon of the technology needs to be factored into the decision as to where to seek patent protection. The attitude of the applicant towards the risks of making a long-term bet on the future prospects of any particular country will also be of influence.

2.3.3
Technology Density

Technology Density and Claim Breadth

If the invention is part of an area of technology that has been the focus of a significant number of patent applications, "claim space" is likely to be rather narrow. The examiner, whose job may be restricted exclusively to a small segment of technology, is likely to be well informed and will easily identify areas of overlap with the state of the art, or claims of questionable inventive step. Indeed, examiners may be exposed to more information in the particular field than inventors.

Areas of high technological density therefore pressure applicants to file patents with rather narrow claims. Broader claims in such areas may carry a higher risk of prolonged discussion with the examiners, causing higher legal fees, delayed patent grant and protection. On the other hand, in exchange for this risk and investment, broad claims covering extensive technology in a densely patented area may be very valuable if granted and enforced. Filing relatively broad claims may therefore be only acceptable to a certain set of applicants with the suitable combination of resources and appetite for risk.

In less technologically dense areas, an applicant may have reason to believe that the invention in question is groundbreaking or at least placed in a field with little ongoing patenting activity. In such situation, filing relatively broad claims may be possible.

Technology Density and the Route of Filing

As well as defining claim breadth, technology density has a direct bearing on the pathway of filing, particularly the timing of resource commitment. As has been identified, patenting strategies can, to a certain degree, elect either the early or late commitment of funds (see Fig. 2.1).

The standard "slow" route comprises filing one application initially, waiting the full 12 months before filing a follow-up application under the PCT procedure and then deciding where to file at the end of the PCT deadline, 30 months after the initial application. Most of the costs of filing are incurred at the end of the 30-month period.

The "fast" route is to simultaneously file applications in as many jurisdictions as one ultimately plans to have a patent in. The sizeable costs of translations, international filing fees and attorney fees occur at the very beginning of the patenting process. Whilst this route may lead to quickly issued patents it introduces the risk that funds are committed before it is clear whether the invention is indeed patentable.

The risk inherent in patenting can never be entirely mitigated, even by diligent searching. Patent applications are usually not published until 18 months after the initial filing, so only at 18 months after the filing of one's own patent, can a full assessment of all possible conflicting prior art and competing patents be made. In areas of high technological activity in which the applicant is seeking broad claims, the number, diversity and density of patent applications increases this risk. This risk profile must be taken into account when choosing between fast and slow application pathways so as to efficiently time the investment of financial resources.

2.3.4
The Commercialisation Plan

The commercial plan for generating profit from a patent goes a long way to define the patent strategy. If the applicant will use the patent in a defined product, the market conditions for which are known, consideration of the conditions imposed by product and market will lead to a fairly clear pathway of patenting. Much of patent strategy however is centred on addressing uncertainties in the commercialisation plan, creating flexibility and value, without conferring significant costs.

Uncertainty

If the applicant has little information about the commercialisation of the eventual patent, there will be a tendency to retain options, so as to not to give away possible opportunities of generating revenue. This uncertainty takes the form of ambiguity as to the likely success of the invention, its potential market, timing of success and geographic market. Established businesses will tend to have a clearer vision of products and markets than entrepreneurial inventors in their first venture. Institutions trying to commercialise the inventions generated by academic researchers need to anticipate the needs of potential licensees or buyers.

Applying for patents in many countries and formulating broad claims may enable the applicant's invention to find its way into a range of as yet unforeseen markets and products. Expectations and uncertainties of this kind are very common.

In the face of this uncertainty a tendency will exist to delay the decision and expense about where to patent as far into the future as possible. The PCT application pathway offers an enormous advantage in this regard, as it allows the applicant to wait almost 30 months, for some jurisdictions extended to 31 months, to take the decision where to file (see Fig. 2.1).

In many fields of commerce and technology, 30 months is a short time in which to significantly increase the certainty of a commercial plan. Since development of the patented invention will often be ongoing after an initial application until beyond the priority period, the real interval during which commercialisation plans must become concrete may be closer to 18 months or shorter. In many industries, licences may take longer than 12 months to negotiate. In any regard, even following the long pathway via PCT creates only a relatively short window in which to create the organisational and financial structures to commercialise ones patent application.

As any change in filing strategy or changes to the application may cause costs later in the patenting process, an applicant is well advised to discuss uncertainty openly with the agent or attorney.

The Scope of Protection

It is in the interest of the applicant to achieve the maximal extent of protection for any product or process patented. Hence, patent agents will try to file claims with maximal breadth for their clients. Going for wide claims, however, in some cases may entail "probing the waters" of what is allowable to the examiners, and how far the technological territory of competitors can be "invaded" by one's own claims. Such broad claiming brings with it a certain risk of prolonged correspondence with the examiner and late issuance of the patent, with no guarantee of a granted patent. Broad claims, if granted, may attract litigation from competitors.

While claiming broadly is a feasible and commonly practiced tactic, some appli-cants may find it in their interest to consider claiming what is needed as immedi-ate protection in return for a quickly issued patent. If a marketed product or pro-cess is to be protected, the necessary scope of protection may be well defined and this narrow and immediate protection may be acceptable. However, if there are plans to license the invention to a wide range of partners, and this necessitates the blocking of many competing technical solutions in the same field, the policy of protection will need to be broader both in scope of claims and in territorial approach. This entails however, both cost and elevated risk.

2.3.5
The Competition

Competing products and competing organisations will influence the need for pro-tection of the invention and the strategy employed to achieve that protection.

Competing Products

Products or processes competing in the same market will often have similar fea-tures; an applicant patenting one particular feature will be tempted to exclude as much of this competition as possible. Indeed, this intent is the very essence of patenting.

The applicant cannot however, bring existing products under the scope of any new claims; they exist as a part of the prior art. The applicant can, however, spec-ulate about possible ways the competition may take to go "around" the invention and try to block these. Speculations about possible competitive developments are common and much effort in research and patenting is driven by the desire to pre-empt the competition. The resulting applications tend to be broader than a patent on one particular solution. Separate nested applications may have to be filed to achieve this objective if all conceivable competitive solutions do not satisfy the cri-terion of "unity" (see Chapter 3).

Again, the costs of this broad approach to protection must be weighted against its benefits. Broadening claims or even filing separate applications will require greater resources for the patenting effort and, more significantly, for the research effort laying the base for sufficient disclosure of such claims.

It is worth reminding oneself that the invention and the protection conferred to it by a patent must be translated into revenue in a market and that protecting an invention is a tool to raise revenue, and is not an end in itself. Markets are usually defined by technical or psychological needs and desires and not by products or inventions.

These questions must be asked: how likely is it for the competition to achieve an advantage in the market with a product from an unrelated technology that was not sufficiently pre-empted? Is the effort of broadening the scope distracting the applicant from the higher goal of improving market position? May the effort di-rected at a defensive patenting achieve better returns if invested in non-IP activities? It is worth analysing not only the technical aspects of the immediate solution offered by the invention, but also its relevance to the market in question. Extensive use of resources spent on protecting an invention must be justifiable by a corresponding value in market power.

Competing Organisations

The threat of a granted patent is likely to have a bearing on the competition in a market. The size and structure of this competition determines its reaction to competing patents. Smaller established firms may be less likely to litigate because of the associated costs, and may also keep their own applications closer to their immediate needs of protection. Larger corporations may have more stamina for risky expenditure and patent broadly and litigate freely.

Any invasion of competing organisation's central interests may represent an existential threat and trigger extensive litigation in smaller firms, while larger organisations or applicants with a less commercial outlook, such as universities, may take a more relaxed approach.

What may seem an insignificant variation in risk profile to one party, may represent a huge threat to another, and tip the scales towards litigation. An applicant may include a marginally broader claim and thus improve the potential value of his patent by a small percentage. But if this broadening of scope threatens a vital business interest of a competitor, that competitor may be forced to do everything possible to invalidate the patent in its entirety. The applicant may thus find that increasing the value of the patent by 5% secured a 100% chance of protracted litigation and a possibility of having the entire application revoked or invalidated. A more focused claim may have been acceptable to the competitor, adverse to the risk and expense of litigation and not existentially threatened by the focussed claim.

The attitude and response of third parties in this "patent game theory" is difficult to predict however. Indeed even in the same technical fields, applicants may chose different patenting strategies to suit their individual situation, and that, at best, qualitative assumptions can be made to competitive responses to new patents.

2.4
Financial Resources and Attitude Towards Risk

None of the scenarios sketched out here offer clear-cut choices between a better and a worse way of patenting. The option of broad or focused claims, fewer or more territories, fast or slow-track examination is a choice between risks of different magnitude and quality. Even in purely rational subjects, the attitude towards risk and reward will be greatly dependent on their circumstances. A commonly used example is shown in Box 4.

> **Box 4**
>
> Suppose that similar offers are made to different companies. The company is invited to make repeated investments of one million, with a ninety percent chance of losing the investment and a ten percent chance of gaining twenty million. Although the risk of losing is large every time, the expected average return is twice the initial investment.
>
> Let us suppose that a small company would be bankrupt after losing one million. Its director could not rationally accept the offer. A large corporation, however, could play as many times as it would take to achieve the average return, effectively doubling the invested money for as long as the offer lasts.
>
> The risk is the same to both players, but their financial background will make their attitude towards that risk, and their resulting response, very different.

Broad claims and geographically expansive applications present elevated risk with greater potential reward. Such strategies are easier to shoulder by larger companies or wealthy applicants with strong financial foundations. Similarly litigation, which is potentially far more costly than application, can be contemplated more easily by players with a higher tolerance and appetite for risk.

The balancing of risk and reward in a patenting strategy is thus a function of the financial resources of the applicant, and other individual factors influencing attitude towards risk (a start-up venture may chose to run a much higher risk profile than a family concern in the fourth generation).

Readers are encouraged to understand their own perceptions and attitudes to the risks of their patent strategy, in light of their financial resources, and to make conscious, rational decisions.

2.5
Business Brief

In order to formulate a coherent patenting strategy, clear objectives need to be stated that serve the applicant's ultimate business interest.

Factors such as
- the technology field,
- the nature of the product in which the invention is used,
- the size and type of the applicant's business,
- the nature of the competition will have an influence on the particular way an application is drafted and pursued in order to meet those objectives.

Important variables that the applicant can employ to adapt the filing strategy to the needs of the particular business are
- where the application is filed first,

- whether an examination is requested early and the patentability of the claims is validated by a patent office,
- by what pathway later filings are submitted to what offices,
- how much technical area the claims cover in relation to the immediate need of protection of the applicant's business.

An outside investor will obtain valuable insight into how well a particular patent or entire IP portfolio is adapted to the needs of a business by considering these issues. Furthermore, adapting this way of looking at IP issues will also shed light on the management responsible for shaping the IP structure of a business.

3
Patenting

Claas Junghans

This chapter is concerned with the process of transforming the results of research into a valid and valuable patent family. Ideally research is performed with the needs of the patenting process in mind, with a clear understanding of the competitive environment of the planned development and of the freedom to operate granted by the scope of existing patents. IP generation is rarely the only consideration to drive research however, and innovation, by its nature, occurs in an unscheduled fashion. Nevertheless incorporation of the patent process into research is of great benefit in making the process cost-effective. "Thinking patents" is a hollow business idiom until the entire machinery of IP generation is an integral part of the overall business process, from a project's initiation to its conclusion. The additional expense of this integrated approach is more than offset by its advantages; granted applications, reduced legal fees and minimised litigation.

This chapter addresses how to progress from poorly defined investigation to a rigorously researched and defined patent. As is emphasised throughout this book, this owes as much to basic planning and economic reasoning, as it does to excellent legal technique and management of the formalities. Scientific research and technical development is many times as expensive as patenting, and this focus on careful planning can equally be applied to the field of research leading up to invention. Patenting is an extension of this inventive process, and the fewer errors that are introduced into the pipeline, the lower the downstream costs. Rigour, forward thinking, and continual review are universally cost-effective business tools.

3.1
Preparation

Whilst an invention is made by an inventor, responsibility for patenting lies with the applicant. Mechanisms of patent right transfer, modalities of employee-invention regulations and the issue of invention theft are treated in Chapter 4. Although it is to the applicant that this chapter therefore predominantly addresses itself, in the interests of coherence, it is important that the technical expertise of the inventor is retained throughout the patent process.

Intellectual Property Management. Claas Junghans, Adam Levy
Copyright © 2006 WILEY-VCH Verlag GmbH & Co. KGaA, Weinheim

3.1.1
Planning

Once it is suggested that a patentable invention has been made, the applicant needs to draw up a plan as to how to proceed, paying particular attention to the costs of the application. An important postulate of IP generation is that the certainty of costs should be balanced by the plausibility and scale of revenue. It will often not be possible to make accurate forecasts of sales or licence fees on future products or technologies, yet an approximation, however imperfect, should initially be made.

To be economically meaningful, this approximation will be inclusive of both direct costs such as attorney and office fees, and also indirect costs such as management time, prototyping, marketing and business development. The cost model should be based on a cost of capital that incorporates the applicant's approach to risk, and this model will look very different to an established business with a strong history of patenting, than to a lone but brilliant inventor. The patent-knowledgeable and cash-generative business has attorneys at hand, an established internal patent process and is able to consider the net value of a patent or invention with relative immunity from the obligation of short-term cashflow.

The lone inventor or start-up company must focus attentively on their cash position as well as on overall value. Remaining cashflow positive throughout patent drafting, license negotiating and potential prosecution takes considerable management resource. Entrepreneurial myopia and a lack of experience means that the lone inventor is very much more likely to miscalculate this cost-revenue balance, or indeed to perform no calculation at all.

As a consequence of unrealistic commercial expectations and poor budgeting, unsupported inventors frequently abandon applications relatively early in the patent process. Ironically this typically occurs at the EP stage, when the patentability of the invention has been established but the cost of transfer to national offices becomes overwhelming. The applicant is left with both financial loss and the disappointment that the invention will not be commercialised.

This emphasises the importance of continual reassessment of the cost-benefit balance. Initial calculations may be imprecise but will become successively more meaningful as new market, competitive and technological information emerges. The applicant must be careful both to perform this forecast and to respect its result; "sunk costs", expenses that have already been incurred are not relevant in valuing continued development and application.

3.1.2
Assembling Material

If this planning determines that a patent application should proceed, the applicant should gather and sort as much relevant data as possible. The eventual application will detail the invention itself, but data relating to competing or associated technology should be factored into the drafting process. Not all material will necessarily end up in the application, but the late introduction of information adds significantly to the expense of patent application.

The objective of the patenting process is a clear definition of the invention against a well-researched background of prior art. The material assembled at this stage can thus be divided into two groups: data positively describing the invention, and data which delineates what was known before the invention, thus forming the state of the art and defining the "space of patentability". A detailed understanding of competing and related technology distinguishes the invention from what is the state of the art, and thus optimizes the chance of obtaining a strong and valid patent.

Material Describing the Invention
In a first step, the "positive" data describing the invention is gathered. This material comprises the abstract idea of the inventor, its concrete manifestations or "embodiments" as laboratory examples or technical drawings, ideas as to how the abstract invention may additionally be used or embodied and speculative excursions into the realm of what may be possible but not yet realized.

Hard data and examples   All data, examples and drawings that exemplify and illustrate the invention should be presented, even if the inventor believes them to be redundant or overlapping. Differences between examples or manifestations of an invention may represent as-yet unseen inventive elements that would otherwise be lost.

Examples and hard data ultimately form the backbone of the description on which subsequently claims rely. Data also demonstrates the extent to which the inventor had the invention in hand at the day of filing. This may be particularly important during US "interference" procedures. During drafting the inclusion of examples will need to be balanced against the application length, in order to minimise translation costs. In the collection phase, however, all data should be included and assessed.

Abstractions   The inventor or applicant can include a generalisation of, or the abstract principle behind the concrete examples of the invention. Whether or not the "idea" behind the invention will become a claim depends on the existing prior art.

Planned future developments   An important part of the material collection is the plan for future developments of the invention. How can the invention be improved further? What elements could be added? Are these developments already attainable or is further R&D activity needed, and if so, can an estimate be made of the time and cost of development and of its likelihood of success?

All ideas and plans should be discussed with the attorney, but not all of these will be included in the draft. It is important though, for the attorney to understand the future direction of research in order to outline a patent strategy that goes beyond the application at hand. On the other hand, weak description of unsubstantiated potential inventions may render future applications vulnerable. The current patent itself may not sufficiently disclose the future invention, but the publication of a future development may expose a subsequent patent to the attack of obviousness.

Ranges   At some point, the attorney drafting the application will ask about the necessity of any specific element of the invention: can it be done without the little wheel in the lower left corner? If an angle of 60 degrees works, would 75 degrees work as well? The better an applicant can provide this detail, the stronger and broader the patent. The more this kind of question can be pre-empted and information provided upfront to the attorney, the less time and money will be spent on correspondence.

The process of gathering this evidence need not be onerous, particularly if the inventor maintains good lab books or drawings. It is important to collect this information diligently before seeing the attorney, rather than sending subsequent additional material, increasing cost and frustration.

Competing or Surrounding Technologies

The technologies forming the competitive environment define the closest state of the art, and allow the attorney to factor the technical and economical environment of the invention into the wider patenting strategy.

The closest state of the art   This is a technical term of patent law. In order to define the invention, the disclosure needs to identify the product or process that is technically closest to the invention. The difference between this "closest state of the art" and the invention defines the "objective of the invention", and acquires a lot of meaning in the context of obviousness. It may also play a role in determining later infringement by others, particularly if the alleged infringer is using "equivalents"; that is elements that are similar but not quite the same as the claimed invention.

Competing technology   Innovations that are not technologically the closest relative to the invention but which are likely to compete with it in the marketplace are also an important consideration in drafting. They help the attorney to accentuate the economically relevant features of the invention and to formulate strategies that anticipate changes in the competitive landscape.

3.1.3
Researching the Literature

The process of searching and finding the competing and surrounding technologies that define the state of the art is an enormously important one, and its successful completion requires training and experience. This "training and experience" almost always translates into cost, but there are different approaches that applicants can take depending on budget.

- Applicants can perform a search by themselves. This means researching databases to check whether any of the elements of the invention, or the invention in its entirety, are already known to the public.
- On the basis of this search, the applicant can submit an application to a patent office and request a search procedure, which invariably is anyway part of the patent process. Some offices perform searches quickly and cheaply. They will, however, only search the literature for claims submitted in the application, and not on the invention disclosed more broadly in the description.
- A professional search can be commissioned from a suitable provider. Commercial search agents can be found by internet search engines, in the regional yellow pages of larger communities and through the growing network of governmental technology support agencies.

Even if a professional search is chosen, it is recommended that applicants familiarize themselves with the search process to some extent. The search for prior art entails the exploration of technical, scientific and patent databases to establish whether the invention has previously been published. Inventors are likely to be familiar with the technical and scientific databases in their inventive field, but less conversant with patent databases.

Patent Databases

Patent literature is a world of its own, rich in its own language and symbolism. Apart from the immense wealth of technical information contained in patents, they also engender a cultural fascination. Few sources of literature are so clearly written with money in mind, which may make patent archives one of the more telling reflections of our age. Patent databases may be conveniently accessed through the Internet or through CD/DVD ROM archives, available in patent offices or depositories and some large libraries. A long list of patent information resources can be found on the EPO website.

Several extensive patent databases are freely available on the Internet. The websites of the European Patent Office, the United States Patent and Trademark Office and most national patent office websites offer free search tools, but care must be taken to distinguish between the website of access (e.g. the EPO, the UK office) and the database itself. Access is restricted to the large and comprehensive patent database, INPADOC, but many of its features are referenced in *Espacenet*, a database project of the European Patent Office and many national offices. Espacenet allows free access to a very large body of patent literature and is available in several languages.

In many technical areas, during the prior art search the fastest way to understand a document is to study its figures and diagrams. Unfortunately drawings are the least accessible parts of the freely available web information, and technical figures in pdf format can be downloaded only page by page, and not by every browser. The USPTO site is a laudable exception but contains only US patents. This may seem a minor impediment at the initial stage of a prior art search, but for regular literature access or for more extended searches, the commercial alternatives should be considered

The formerly-free IBM patent website has matured into the fee-based, patent search-engine Delphion, which offers a download capability for pdf documents and convenient features such as search files and forward references. As a free alternative several programmes exist to circumvent the restriction to single-page downloads. Some patent offices officially discourage the use of such programmes, but one would hope that the future will bring more widely available free downloads, as patent offices become increasingly user-friendly.

Some patent offices offer consulting to first-time inventors; the German office has a very popular service and performs exemplary searches at the offices and on-line. Readers with easy access to a national patent office may also benefit from staff assistance at the on-site search facilities there. A list of addresses of the European national offices can be found on the EPO website.

How to Search
Many databases link patent documents and history, and a good initial search will often open the way to find a series of related documents. The first challenge though is to get a foot in the door. Different search terms may prove effective:
- technical terms,
- inventor names,
- applicant / assignee names,
- patent classification.

The careful use of logical operators ensures the return of a manageable yet meaningful number of search results. When "steam cooker" is inserted into the search field, interpretation as "steam" AND "cooker" will bring up predominantly the device used as an example in Chapter 1, whereas "steam" OR "cooker" will swamp the desired result in a sea of inventions relating either to *steam* or *cooking* alone. Indeed familiarisation with the specific query language of any database will greatly improve the results. The Boolean operator "near", for example, is great help in searching for documents in which two common generic terms occur in proximity in a large volume of text. Many databases contain their own idiosyncratic operators, and care must be taken to use the right operators for the database.

Searching for inventor names is useful when trying to make a connection from a scientific paper to the patent literature, and when little additional information about the likely scope of the patent is available.

Particularly when an invention has emerged from academia or in collaboration with academics, one is well advised to look thoroughly for scientific publications by the academic collaborators. Many scientists are oriented toward publication, and may be unaware of the absolute requirement of non-disclosure before filing an application.

While searching for technical terms or names is straightforward, the system of patent classification requires a short explanation.

Patent classification systems The International Patent Classification (IPC) assigns all inventions to at least one of eight classes, labelled A to H, reflecting the 19th century division of technology. These main classes in turn are divided into subclasses, which again contain subclasses, and so forth. The WIPO website has in-depth information about patent and other IP classification systems.

The Espacenet search engine uses a closely related European classification system, ECLA, and the USPTO, yet another classification system. Each is explained on the relevant website.

Steam cookers, to continue the example, are found in IPC and ECLA class A47 J27. The hierarchy is

A   Human necessities
A4   Personal or domestic articles
A47   Furniture, appliances, coffee mills, suction cleaners
A47J   Kitchen equipment
A47J 27   Cooking vessels.

Similarly, a genetically engineered mouse is at home in ECLA A01K67/027A1. The common denominator is that both steam cookers and genetically engineered mice are human necessities, at least in the eyes of the patent office. It will take generations of cultural anthropologists to understand the phylogenetic tree of our technology.

The search by patent class is helpful when the key word searches do not capture the relevant documents or identify an excess of documents. Generic terms can be used to look for possible IPCs that may contain inventions relating to the search terms. Since patent examiners indicate the classes searched in a formal search or examination (see the search report example in Chapter 1), looking for any particular class or combination of classes can be a powerful tool to highlight documents which are not otherwise connected to the invention.

References and families A feature of commercial sites is the ability to perform quick family searches and to check upwards and downwards through references and citations. This is a very convenient tool to widen the search once a closely related document has been found.

If a patent document is found that closely relates to the applicant's invention, but does not completely pre-empt it, the applicant should now start to worry that the author of the document may have disclosed material even closer to the invention in another application, for instance in a follow-up PCT application. Since all documents related by a common priority form one "family" in the cosy terms of patent language, they will appear in the database and can be quickly accessed. The document may also have been used as technical background for other applications that pre-empt the invention. It is likely that the document will be cited in these subsequent applications.

Literacy in database mining is a feature of digital life today and any reader would be better served by spending time performing several searches and exploring the network of patent databases, than reading lengthy explanations here. A few hours thus invested will give great insight into the features and advantages of the different databases.

What to Look For

At this early preliminary stage, the applicant is involved with finding documents that relate closely to the topic of the invention and whether these documents refer to patents in force or abandoned is not important. Any prior documents that describe the invention, or parts of it, are relevant to patentability and should be presented to the attorney preparing the draft. The primary concern is to find prior art that destroys the novelty of the invention; a publication that describes all the "elements" of the invention in one embodiment.

It is important to stress that only the combination of all the inventive elements in one embodiment destroys novelty, so the applicant should not concede defeat prematurely even if all the elements are already separately published. For example, if an application relates to a genetically engineered mouse with a 75 cm tail which is green, the prior publication of a mouse with a brown 75 cm tail, and another mouse with a normal length, green tail would not destroy its novelty. The examiner may question the inventive step but that is another question. And yes mice can be patented, meet them in ECLA A01K67/027 !

Nor is the identification of prior art which pre-empts the planned application necessarily reason to completely abandon an application. Often, the invention may contain elements that are not pre-empted in the prior art, and whilst the scope of the patent may be altered, a valid patent may emerge in discussion with an attorney. It must be realised however that such pre-emption is likely to reduce the range of protection, and may enable ways around the invention. The economic equation of cost, value and risk will need to be again assessed.

Find your own fault   This search amounts to the applicant trying to poke holes in the application before it is even drafted. This may seem paradoxical to many applicants, yet it is very much in the applicant's interest. The patent will be examined at some stage and the examiner is likely to find any prior art. In this event the application will be refused or after a considerable delay will be issued with its scope limited by this prior art. Identifying prior art in advance of examination makes the process faster and cheaper, and leads to stronger patents.

Some applicants may bet on the examiner being short on time, or not having the knowledge to find a certain piece of prior art due to special circumstances, and in all fairness, this does occur. The result is a formally examined patent, some or all of the claims of which may be latently unpatentable. This patent may be of some value to the applicant, since there are immediate legal consequences in a granted patent. The competition however, after performing its own search will identify prior art and attack the patent by opposition or revocation proceedings against the frivolous applicant. Any valuable patent will be submitted to a search by competitive companies, prior art will be unearthed, and only clean patents will prevail. These companies however, based on their own risk-return models, may decide not to bear the cost of this process, and may chose to turn a blind eye to such patents. There is some motivation therefore, for trying to pass unpatentable matter by the examiner, but this is a strategy that should be discussed in detail with the attorney, and one that is rarely adopted by small companies or lone inventors.

In some jurisdictions the submission of claims that are, to the knowledge of the patentee, not patentable, may result in loss of the patent and can expose the patentee to prosecution.

Structuring the search   A positive finding that prior art exists and the invention is not patentable without limitation of scope is a definitive finding. A negative finding however, meaning that the invention is not part of the prior art, is never definitive. In the words of a recent US Secretary of Defence, "Absence of evidence is not evidence of absence".

Searching for prior art means looking for something one does not want to find. Following a preset script of keywords, competing inventors, applicants and companies will help to avoid falling into the psychological traps of prematurely stopping the search, or indeed of endless searching. Whilst the competition damaged by a commercially successful patent may make lengthy efforts to identify prior art, the applicant must be pragmatic, ending the search when satisfied that the enquiry is sufficiently thorough.

Professional Searches
Depending on the result of the preliminary search, the budget and the experience of the applicant, a professional service may be commissioned to perform a search. Professional search agencies are easy to find on the Internet, and some patent office web sites also have listings of commercial search agents.

The European Patent Office offers a "special search service". Within this service searches are conducted by the same professionals that perform searches within the application process, and at the same price. The EPO requires the search to be submitted in the context of a filing, either at a national office or the EPO itself. If this service is used, and the application is later used to claim priority, a refund is given on the search fee of the subsequent EP application.

Be aware however, that the search service offered by the EPO is directed towards specific claims, and not towards the patentability of the subject matter disclosed in the description.

Patent attorneys may also be willing to perform professional searches. Some attorneys view commissioned searches as a port of entry to new clients, whilst others resist performing searches for applications that they are to draft because of liability concerns.

Indeed an applicant should consider the different options before instructing an attorney to both research and draft an application. There is a clear conflict of interest between the need to diligently search for and find prior art, and the desire to charge fees for an application if prior art is not found. As a result, some attorneys do tend to be rather optimistic as to the patentability of inventions, and there is certainly evidence of applicants being persuaded to file applications based on less-than-stringent searches. A long-standing relationship with a trusted attorney may make such concerns unfounded, but unless you know and trust your attorney separate search and filing is highly recommended.

Documenting Searches

Given the expense and time involved in a search, it is important that the search method, terms and results are thoroughly documented. This gives the applicant documentary evidence of the patent terrain, and permits a return to important topics, inventors and patent families. Good search documentation strengthens the applicant's position with investors and clients in the absence of a formal examination.

I have seen several large invoices for searches that rendered only a handful of vaguely related documents, in which the searchers claimed to have looked at several hundred documents without finding conflicting prior art. The invoices gave few details as to how the search was performed or what documentary terrain was covered. One is left to wonder whether the client would accept a similarly non-specific bill from their car mechanic.

3.2
Drafting the Patent Application

Many applications will be drafted by attorneys rather than applicants, and it is worth considering the issues that surround hiring and instructing an attorney, and the technical issues that are likely to emerge during drafting discussions.

3.2.1
Attorneys

Armed with a thoroughly conducted financial model, the results of a preliminary patent search, and a collated portfolio of relevant documents, the next step is to find and hire a patent attorney to draft the application.

Whether and How to Hire an Attorney

Patent attorneys, also known as patent agents, patent lawyers or professional representatives, come from either a technical or legal background. They perform services in the fields of patent drafting, prosecution and defence as well as related work such as registering design patents and trademarks, structuring attacks on competitors' portfolios and giving opinion on freedom-to-operate. Drafting is usually performed by professionals with a background in science or engineering, ideally in the field of the invention.

Whilst it is clear that an attorney is essential to defend against the accusation of patent infringement and to attack competing patents in court, it is tempting to believe that drafting and submitting patents can be achieved without the additional cost of an attorney. Successfully filing valid and valuable applications, however, requires experience, diligence and time. Although it is possible to complete such an application without the help of an attorney, making a mistake is a costly way of learning, and there are several mistakes that once made, can not be undone. Indeed, it is unlikely that, however technologically knowledgeable, the inventor-applicant will have the technical legal knowledge to make strongly worded claims, and to successfully prosecute the application. Unless the applicant has significant experience in writing and prosecuting patents a professional needs to be employed. Simply put, a patent attorney will cost money, but can generate a lot of value.

This said, many inventors become frustrated by paying high fees and receiving what they perceive as little added value during the course of submitting an application through a patent attorney. Having looked closely at a few such complaints, some may be justified. There is no clear formula to avoid this frustration, but some components of a successful client-attorney relationship can be identified:

- Personal references. Do not rely on fame or second-hand opinion; find people who have actually done business with a particular attorney. Was the filing successful? Were there any surprises, especially regarding the financial aspects of the relationship?
- Experience. Look for an attorney who has experience in the field of the invention. People or businesses working in the industry, but who are not competitors will give the most objective references. Do not expect your attorney to be familiar with your particular corner of research, but to have experience in the technical field.
- Reference other patents. In the absence of client references, find out the IPC of the invention and look up some applications. The attorneys or agents who handled the application will be named in the priority application. Contacting the applicant, who is also named on the cover sheet, may be one way to get a reference on the attorney.
- Be realistic. If you are an applicant with a limited record of applications, realize that if approaching a large firm, your invention is unlikely to be the sole interest of a senior partner. More likely, you are going to be dealing with a junior with less experience.

This is not at all bad news if, as is likely, the relative novice does a good job, and you are not compelled to pay for the hours of a senior partner.

- Be commercial. Realise that you are in a business relationship. Bring up the issue of cost and openly state your expectations. Be prepared to walk away from a relationship that does not meet any realistic and justifiable expectations.
- Preparation. If technical, economic and legal needs can be communicated well, the attorney will be in a good position to give advice tailored to the situation. Be aware that much of the unnecessary cost and frustration in the attorney-client relationship can be attributed to an insufficient flow of information. Patent attorneys are amongst the highest paid consultants that a small company hires, and complete information allows them to leverage their skills and to utilise efficiently their time on the applicant's behalf.

With careful preparation, and with the basic knowledge contained within this and the preceding chapters, an applicant close to the field of the invention will be able to provide a structured and succinct description of the invention with which a patent attorney can generate an application in less than a day. If this is not the case, the basis of the fee and ways to improve the efficiency of the relationship might be profitably discussed with the attorney.

3.2.2
The Initial Filing as a Basis for Amended Claims

Applicants do wonder at the large size and inherent redundancy of many descriptions, and the apparent difference between the description and the claims. Often the reason for these phenomena is that the initially filed description is intended to support, if necessary, a future modification of claims.

According to the philosophy of patent law, the right of exclusion is granted in return for the disclosure made by the inventor. The description gives the background of the claims and supports their interpretation. Hence, anything that the applicant wants to claim needs to be elaborately described in the description. In many technical areas, the invention will be discussed from a range of points of view and in different levels of abstraction, relating to the different breadths of the claims. Examples of embodiments of the invention will also be included in the description to support specific claims.

The content of an application at the time of filing forms the first part of the Patent Office file for the invention, and therefore defines what will become publicly disclosed, even if some of the text is later deleted. It is important to realise that the applicant will be able to modify the claims during prosecution, but that there is no opportunity to add substantive matter to the application that was not contained at the time of filing.

If the priority of the first application is subsequently used to file another application, more substantive matter may be added, but this matter will receive a later "time stamp". In any event, adding substance through a second filing is only possible within the twelve months of priority.

During the examination process, the patent office will often come up with documents that were not found during the initial search conducted by the applicant or the attorney. Examiners often have access to more documents than the applicant, and they are highly trained to identify prior art. "Prior rights" may also exist in the form of applications that were unpublished at the time of application, but were filed awaiting publication. Such prior rights may impact on the patentability of initially submitted claims.

If such prior art or prior rights emerge during the examination process, the claims will have to be amended. New claims can only be drafted on the basis of the content of the initially submitted description. This emphasises the need to state clearly everything that is important about the invention, even if not all of the disclosed material may be immediately important to support the initial claims.

If the invention confers any additional technical advantages above and beyond what is described as the problem to be solved, these should be stated clearly. Faster or cheaper ways of production, greater user-friendliness, increased environmental compatibility; any other "side-effect" may be an important support for subsequently altered claims. If prior art makes amending the claims necessary, the problem defining the invention may change.

Whilst these additional advantages may be an important aspect of defining the invention, it should be kept in mind that an application is a legal document and not promotional material. Space should not be wasted on untrue or non-technical advantages of the invention. The requirement of enabling disclosure does, if anything, necessitate mentioning the limitations of the invention. Indeed in the US, this is a standard interpretation of the corresponding section 112 of the US patent law (35 U.S.C.).

Prior art found by the examiner is one reason why claims may have to be amended during the granting process. Applicants themselves may be motivated to change the wording of the claims to shift the focus of the utility of an invention when competing products or technology come to light after the submission of the application, or based on a change in the applicant's perspective or strategy. Modifications of claims are possible until late in the examination and granting process, but only on the basis of initial disclosure.

Another reason to include additional aspects outside of what precisely is claimed is the desire to manifestly state known but not claimed alternatives to the given examples. This documents that the applicant at the time of application was aware of certain equivalents to the main embodiments, and that these equivalents were deemed to fall under the scope of the invention.

Mind the Volume

Material added to the direct descriptions of the claimed invention can be justified, because it lays the foundation of eventual fallback positions. There is no need, however, for lengthy introductions beyond one or two sentences about the field of the invention, a clear description of the closest state of the art and a succinct statement of the problem that the invention solves. Descriptions of mechanical inventions starting with Newton, or biological ones introducing Darwin or Watson-Crick may make nice reading, but such introductions make an application none the stronger, but a lot more expensive.

Patents ultimately require translation into the national languages of the countries in which protection is sought. Average translation costs range from 0.20 € to 0.40 € per word, and an application that is to enter the national phase in all of the members and associated states of the European Patent Convention will need to be translated into more than 20 languages, and this number does not account for markets such as China, Russia, Japan, Korea, Israel, Indonesia or the Arab world[1]. Translation is an important component of the overall cost structure of an application, and ultimately, superfluous words that do not support the strength of the patent add cost without value.

Despite this cost, descriptions are sometimes redundant and overly verbose in their wording. It is not uncommon to find a ninety-page document describing an invention that the applicant described in a brief technical manuscript. What, if any, justification exists for such voluminous description should be discussed with the attorney. There may be good reason for a certain redundancy, but in some cases the lingering suspicion is that much verbosity is directed towards justifying large drafting fees and subsequent translation commissions. Applicants, particularly if the bulk of text consists of definitions, should ensure that this is required. Most technical descriptions are generic, and the "person of average skill in the art" to whom all patent law refers will understand what is meant. Artificial or overly particular expressions should be avoided in the definition of an invention.

The skill and art that goes into the drafting of a patent is not directly correlated to the number of pages in an application. Short succinct applications may be the fruit of long hours and great effort, whilst lengthy documents can be the result of simple copy-paste. Armed with basic knowledge of the process an applicant will be able to ensure that the cost of an application is matched by its quality.

Examples and the Importance of Disclosure

Hypothetical examples   Working examples are the best way for an applicant to show that the invention was in his or her possession at the time of filing. The easiest way to draft an example is to directly transfer data from the lab book or, in

---

1)   Other important countries in the Americas and Africa are covered by translations to the European Patent Convention member state languages, most importantly English, French, Spanish and Portugese. The applications, especially the claims may have to be adapted to the specific national requirements of these countries.

case of a mechanical or electronic invention, from the corresponding technical drawings. The attorney drafting the application will filter most of the information into strongly supportive examples.

Sometimes, the crucial step in making an invention may have been taken, but the details may not have been completed when the decision to draft an application is made. The question as to how "hypothetical" an example should be included is often raised. Indeed, the same question can be applied to the disclosure in general. One may well dream up an invention in detail and submit it, along with a hypothetical example. If the invention and the example works a patent may be granted, but if the hypothetical invention does not work, or the disclosure is insufficiently clear and the person skilled in the art is unable to reproduce the invention from what is disclosed, the patent may be attacked and invalidated. Different jurisdictions have different standards of disclosure, and the applicant is advised to consult the attorney with regard to any particular case.

Another variable in determining the validity of hypothetical examples seems to be the technical field of the invention. From my own experience, hypothetical predictions of experimental outcomes in chemical and biological fields may be discouraged, whilst colleagues from the realm of physics and mechanics seem to be quite happy to rely on paper and pencil in making inventions.

Regardless of the individual situation, the applicant should be aware that only a broad and enabling disclosure will form the basis of a solid patent. On the other hand, including a probable, but hypothetical, example may better serve an applicant than waiting five months for an experimental result and losing a patent to the competition.

Examples disclosing trade secrets   The applicant may find that in describing the way to practice an invention, there may be a need to include information that is not a direct element of the inventive step, but which, in practice, is required to realise the invention. Examples include temperature ranges or quantities of reagents in chemical inventions, ways to treat a surface in nanotechnology and equivalent disclosures in other fields.

Applicants may legitimately feel that they would rather not disclose these non-patentable "tricks of the trade" to their competition. There is no easy answer to this dilemma and it should be discussed in detail with an attorney. One immediate question is whether the technology in question is not a patentable invention in itself, and whether it could therefore form the subject of an unrelated application. The same iterations of searches and cost-value calculations must be performed to find out whether this is the case.

Applicants often suggest using a non-optimal standard example or a hypothetical way of practising the invention without the trade secret. If the application is to be used as a PCT application or as a priority-founding application, the applicants and their attorney should consider whether the proposed solution to the problem does not interfere with so-called "best mode" requirements of US patent law. There, an applicant who submits an application in which the best mode of applying an invention is consciously not included runs the risk of losing the patent in litigation.

It must be considered that for very valuable patents, the competition may well hire an expert and investigate the details of the disclosure in an effort to weaken a patent in the European opposition or revocation process or its international equivalent. Applicants may therefore be more secure making full and complete disclosure.

3.2.3
Non-Obviousness

The two important criteria for material patentability are novelty and non-obviousness. Novelty refers to the question of whether an invention has been anticipated in all of its elements before, and few conscious attempts are made to patent an invention that has been published previously. Much progress however is incremental, and depending on viewpoint, an improvement of a previously known technology may be regarded as a flash of ingenuity by the inventor and their employer, or as an obvious, non-inventive, minor improvement by a competitor.

The outcome of this conflict depends on the particular case and ultimately will be decided by the patent offices and higher courts. A fairly reproducible mechanism however has been established that can be employed to anticipate decisions on obviousness. A method called the "problem-solution approach" is of particular importance in Europe. Formerly put into code as part of the "Guidelines for Examination before the European Patent Office", this method is of use beyond the EPO and may guide applicants in their assessment of whether a particular innovation is inventive and non-obvious.

The "Problem–Solution Approach"

In most cases, the issue of non-obviousness arises when *all* elements of the invention are anticipated by earlier publications but are not anticipated together in a single embodiment. Often several elements are part of one, and other elements are part of another piece of prior art.

To return to the prior example of the innovation of a genetically engineered mouse with a 75 cm long green tail, after previous publication of scientific articles discussing a mouse with a 75 cm long brown tail, and independently, a mouse with a normal length, green tail.

The characterising elements of the disputed claim are "75 cm" and "green". In dispute is whether the combination of the two known elements is inventive. The patent examiner or judge called upon to decide the issue in the above case will perform three formal steps:

- definition of the publication forming the closest piece of prior art,
- objective identification of the technical problem by comparison of the disputed invention to this prior art,
- examination of whether the solution to this technical problem was made obvious by other prior art.

In the example above, two alternative analyses can be made. The closest prior art can be the paper describing a long tail. The problem to be solved by the invention would then be to make a mouse with a green tail. This had previously been described in the second paper, giving support to the argument that the solution to the problem was known. The argument to defend or attack the non-obviousness concentrates on whether the "teaching" of this paper can be adapted to the particular problem. There may be reasons to argue that it was not at all obvious to make a mouse with a green, long tail; for example, long tails could be notoriously difficult to change in colour and the procedure different to the prior art in significant details.

Alternatively, the closest prior art could be the green-tailed mouse, and the objective of the invention to make a long-tailed mouse. Here, the solution had again been anticipated for the same reasoning, and the same test of obviousness can be applied.

There are two key observations:
1. The patent office may define the "objective problem to be solved by the invention" by contrasting the closest prior art with the technical effects of the invention. This definition may be different from the problem defined in the original application.
2. The identification of the closest prior art has a strong bearing on whether the solution offered by the invention is obvious or not.

As a consequence, in situations where the inventiveness of a particular invention is in doubt, proper selection of the closest prior art and statement of the problem to be solved goes a long way in anticipating and pre-empting the reasoning of the examiner.

The "Person Skilled in the Art"
The issue of whether an improvement was obvious at the time of its inception depends on the answer to the question: obvious to whom? Patent law refers to the "person skilled in the art" or its semantic equivalent. Just how skilled, and in what art, depends on the particular jurisdiction and case.

In many cases the invention will be made in a technical field that can be defined easily. The person skilled in the art in that field is someone confronted by the kind of problems solved by the invention, familiar with the literature and practice of the technical field and able to perform small experiments in which known parameters of a process or product are changed within tight limits. The person skilled in the art is able to combine teachings from different publications in the literature.

Small deviations of standard parameters are thus not inventive unless they have a surprising effect. Combining known elements to achieve an effect that similar combinations have previously shown is equally obvious. On the other hand, a new problem for a known solution, surprising effects of a combination of known elements, and extension of known parameter ranges, can all be inventive.

Another level of complexity is approached if an invention crosses the borders of a technical field. Then, depending on the jurisdiction, skilled persons of other technical areas, or even entire teams, may have to be invoked as the imaginary "person skilled in the art".

The topic of non-obviousness is the most ambiguous requirement of patentability, and has been the subject of much dispute. Readers who are interested in learning more about the issue are referred to the respective legal commentaries. The EPO has edited an excellent treatise on the subject in its material on case law before the EPO, available for free on its website.

3.2.4
Unity

In addition to the requirements of novelty and inventiveness, unity is a more formal requirement of a patent. The idea is essentially to avoid issuing patents that contain more than one invention. Unity is attained if all claims of a patent contain one central inventive idea or element.

The attorney drafting the application from the submitted material will try to isolate one essential "idea" or unifying concept of the invention in its greatest abstraction, in order to attain a maximal scope or breadth of protection. Prolific inventors may have disclosed in their briefing, elements that are new and inventive but which cannot rigorously be subsumed under one inventive principle. In doing so, the inventor may consciously or unconsciously have made more than one invention. This is solved by filing more than one application and claiming the inventions separately.

There may be problems with this strategy, though, if both inventions refer to the same examples. The danger exists that one application may disclose aspects claimed in the other application, thus forming a novelty-destroying piece of prior art. This can theoretically be avoided by filing both applications on the same day, but great care would be needed to ensure the physical arrival of the applications the same day, by sending a fax or using the same envelope. A more convenient way is to file one application, and to subsequently segregate the different applications into "divisional applications". This approach also permits fees to be deferred.

Box 5
Unity Example

As an example for a unity conflict, let us return to the steam cooking pot used to illustrate dependency in Chapter 1. This time the inventor of the steam cooker has included a safety valve in the initial application. The principle of the valve may be applicable to many other technical fields, such as chemical engineering, and merit protection on its own.

The applicant initially proposes a claim set to the attorney:

1. Apparatus for the cooking of food comprising a pot (1) and a lid (2), characterized by the lid being fastened to the pot in a steam-tight fashion, creating a chamber (3) that can be pressurized.
2. Steam cooking apparatus comprising a pot and a lid, where the lid is fastened to the pot in a steam tight manner creating a steam-tight chamber, characterized by a safety valve being comprised in one of the enclosures of the steam-tight chamber.
3. Safety valve characterized by a spring-actuated mechanism comprising a steel spring.

The attorney or examiner will tell the applicant that claims 1 and 3 are lacking unity, because there is no inventive element that is common to the two claims. Claim 1 describes a pot, and claim 3 a valve, and only claim 2 has a common inventive idea with both claim 1 and claim 3.

3.3
Prosecution

3.3.1
Formalities

Filing and maintaining the formal requirements of an application requires diligence in execution, if not great intellect, and it is highly recommendable for applicants with few patents to leave the formal side of prosecution to an attorney. Indeed many countries require the applicant to employ a professional representative familiar with the national legal mechanism. The formal requirements of prosecution include the following items.

Fees and Payment

In the absence of professional help proper fee management is an important issue. Depending on the jurisdiction, patent prosecution requires the payment of fees according to a strict schedule. Some jurisdictions still accept cheques, and funds must be cleared in order to meet these fee schedules, and as a result may need to arrive more than one week before the expiry of the corresponding deadline.

The EPO has installed an account system that allows for the almost instant payment of fees from money deposited with the EPO on a current account. This option is of interest to applicants with a large caseload of business with the Office. Fees before the USPTO may be subject to a reduction if the applicant is a small business. Fees relating to search and examination as part of EPO procedures in prosecution of a European Patent Application are reduced if the applicant has performed an earlier, similar action before the EPO as the PCT receiving office.

Deadlines

Actions before an office must usually be performed before a deadline set either by statute or by the office. Failure to act in time may lead to the application being deemed abandoned, or may cause the applicant to lose certain rights. Patent offices, despite their overwhelming workload and subsequent delays, have the serious task of granting market monopoly, and insistence on adherence to a procedural schedule is understandable. Many applicants on the other hand, see an advantage in prolonging procedures to delay the eventual cash-intensive patent issue and publication.

Some deadlines may be missed without compromising the application, and there may be a grace period in which a failure to act or pay on time may be corrected by an additional fee. The European procedure, for instance, allows further processing if an applicant has failed to act on a deadline set by the office. Further recourse is granted in EPO proceedings if the applicant can demonstrate diligence in processing the application and present a good reason for having missed the deadline. This author, for one, would love to see the file of funniest excuses.

The regulations governing patenting procedure vary greatly from one jurisdiction to another, and may be completely different within the same office depending on whether that office acts on it's own behalf or for the PCT pathway. Technicalities such as these make employing an attorney or in-house professional a necessity.

3.3.2
Representation

Depending on the jurisdiction, applicants may be able to act for themselves or may need a professional representative, which in most cases will be a patent attorney or attorney-at-law. As a general rule, most countries allow their own citizens, residents, and legal entities with a place of business in the country, to act without representation before the patent office. This is the case for the European Patent Office. The USPTO requires only a correspondence address in the USA[2], and Britain also allows non-residents to act without representation. Germany requires non-residents to be represented by a patent lawyer or a lawyer. On the other end of the spectrum, Spain requires the applicant to be represented by a patent lawyer, and normal lawyers have no right to represent the applicant before the Spanish Patent and Trademark Office.

The advice regarding attorney selection is especially important in choosing representatives abroad. Researching alternatives and asking for references will go a long way towards reducing the prosecution expenses. One convenient way to handle the application is to ask the "home" attorney to look for and employ col-

---

2) While this author encourages any prospective applicant to seek proper counsel with a patent professional, it needs to be added that particularly in the USA, the Patent Office has a reputation for being helpful and assisting applicants. Applicants who for economic reasons would otherwise have to abandon an application in the US may consider taking the first steps themselves before the USPTO, employing an attorney once they can afford one.

leagues abroad. In many cases, the home attorney will manage the entire case and the client will only pay bills to one attorney. Smaller businesses may find that directly contacting representatives is a more cost-effective approach, and in any case, companies should seek transparent billing from their attorney in dealing with these agents.

3.3.3
The Process

Filing
Once the application has been drafted, the applicant or attorney will send the document to the agreed office. The selection of office and route was discussed in length in Chapter 2.

Applications can be filed by letter, preferably registered letter or messenger, by fax, usually requiring a later submission of the same material by letter, or increasingly, by electronic submission. Care needs to be taken to make the application effective by payment of the related fee.

There may be several motives behind filing an application, particularly a first application. The normal reason is that the applicant wishes to start proceedings before the Patent Office in order to be granted a patent. In this case, very strict adherence to the procedural requirements is advisable, especially if the applicant seeks fast processing of the application.

Another legitimate reason for submitting a first filing is to deposit an official record of an invention, with the plan to later file an improved and adapted application. Initial filing can be used as a "time-stamped" record of an invention, forming the basis of added or modified claims. This may be useful in technology areas in which the applicant would rather not risk being pre-empted by a competitive patent, or in which publication of the invention in a public journal, or at a conference, is pending.

Different jurisdictions provide mechanisms to manage this situation. The EPC, for example, has rather minimal requirements for a European application; in essence, the office needs the name of the applicant, a clear statement that a patent is sought, the nomination of at least one EPC country, and a description and one claim, which may later be modified. The EPO will issue an application number and recognize an application date on the application, even if the formal requirements of a regular application are not met. The USPTO offers an especially pragmatic solution, and under extreme time pressure, an attorney should be able to file an "emergency application" securing maximal scope of protection within the same day.

Designation of Countries in Supranational Pathways
When filing an application through the PCT pathway or before the European Patent Office, the applicant will have to designate the countries in which the application becomes effective. The PCT or EP application is only effective for the countries that are expressly named in the initial application. In both the EP and PCT paper and electronic forms, the standard format designates all member states of

the respective treaty. As a consequence, if the applicant does not actively exclude any specific countries, all countries possible are designated.

Almost any action in the patenting process is accompanied by a fee and this is true for designating countries in the PCT or EPC process. The PCT and EP applications require the payment of seven and five designation fees respectively to cover the designation of all member states. The applicant then has until the national phase in case of a PCT application, or until after the grant of the EP patent, to decide in which countries to continue the application. At the time of entering the national phases a great deal of national fees, translation costs and representative's fees will have to be paid, and the applicant may rightly elect not to continue the application in all member countries.

Publication

18 months after the initial submission, or "priority filing", of an application, the application and all its "daughter" applications in other countries will be published by the respective offices[3]. This means that the initial application will become part of the prior art on the day of publication, with particular relevance to the novelty and obviousness of subsequent applications. This has several consequences:

1. A competitor will have to distinguish a competing invention filed on the day of publication or later, from this new state of the art.
2. The applicant will be confronted with the disclosure of the initial application in later filings of subsequent related inventions. A follow-up invention will be examined independently, even if invented and registered by the same inventor and applicant, and if the follow-up invention is held to be obvious in light of the previously published application it will not be granted.
3. The invention becomes public knowledge, and the competition may profit from this disclosure. The competition will be enabled to start working on improvements, ways around, and ways to fence-in the applicant, probably well before the patent is issued.

If the wish is to create a technical barrier for closely related inventions, the applicant may elect to publish the application as soon as possible. This can be achieved by simply requesting publication from the respective office, or indeed by posting a copy of the disclosure on the applicant's internet site confirmed by a public notary[4]. Asking

---

3) The United States of America used to not publish applications until the patent issued; this practice was changed in the 1990s and today, all US applications are also published after 18 months.

4) Some jurisdictions require *written* disclosure for a publication to be novelty-destroying. Whether a publication on an internet site constitutes such written disclosure may be the subject of debate for some time in some countries.

the patent office to publish an application early grants the applicant the preliminary protection conferred by a published, but unexamined, application.

The applicant, on the other hand, may decide to abandon an application in order to avoid public disclosure. An application can be abandoned and not published until the technical preparations for publication are concluded, about 6 weeks prior to expiry of the 18-month deadline of publication, depending on jurisdiction.

In abandoning the application however, the priority of the initial filing is lost. Although an unpublished application may be subsequently filed again, all or some of its elements may in the meantime have been pre-empted by a competitor, or published in a journal, challenging its patentability. Care must also be taken to abandon all related applications in different countries, since the continued prosecution of one will lead to a publication, rendering the invention unpatentable elsewhere.

This said, reasons may exist for an applicant to abandon an application as part of a strategy to file the same application later with added subject matter.

Examination

Depending on the jurisdiction, the application will either be automatically submitted to examination, or the applicant will have to request examination. The office will often issue a search report prior to the deadline for submission of this request, enabling the applicant to estimate the likelihood of receiving a positive reply.

Examination, as well any search report issued, always refers to the set of claims submitted. The applicant may have an opportunity to change the claims in response to the search or examination report issued by the office. The EPO also allow the applicant to change or amend claims if the examination report is positive and the initially submitted claims are patentable.

If the office issues a negative response, a correspondence will ensue between the office and the applicant or the applicant's representative. The applicant may request a hearing to discuss matters with the examiner, and may call experts to assist in these hearings. The applicant may also be allowed to submit further evidence in forms of examples, experimental results and similar material to demonstrate the particular effect of the invention. This evidence will not however become part of the application upon which amended claims can be based, and will not be given the time stamp of the initial application. Proceeding regulations and the style in which they are conducted vary greatly between jurisdictions.

A principle of modern government is that there should be recourse against decisions made by authorities, and different jurisdictions satisfy this requirement in different ways. Patent law, the subject matter and patent office procedures are exotic to most mainstream law professionals, and the outcome of such appeal proceedings greatly depends on the familiarity of the deciding party with patent procedure. Whilst countries with a long history of patent law have very competent specialized patent courts, applicants may find that recourse is less satisfactory in other countries.

The European Patent Office is a supranational entity upon which no national courts are competent to rule. Nevertheless there is an appeal procedure within the EPO. The PCT pathway has no immediate pathway of recourse, since it does not entail legally binding examination procedures. A disputed decision by the office processing the PCT application can later be appealed before the national offices after nationalisation of the application.

3.4
Strategy

3.4.1
Overview

Previously throughout this book patenting has been described as a rather static process, by which a completed invention is protected legally under carefully planned economical objectives. On the level of an individual application, this approach is justified and productive.

An invention however is rarely an isolated singular occurrence, but the outcome of an ongoing process. This process may generate not one but several patentable results. The question arises how to optimally structure the protection of the results of an ongoing process.

The tools offered by the patent system to respond to a dynamic process of invention are not very versatile. Fixed time limits govern the process, and can only be by-passed at the cost of vastly increased risk to the protection of the invention. Instead of adapting the formalities of protection to the pace of invention, the pace of invention must be changed to adapt to the requirements of patenting.

This issue is therefore essentially reduced to the question of how to fit the development of an invention into the time lines of the patenting process. While this may be a trivial concern to large and established businesses, for a start-up company the correct management of this triangle of development, patenting and financing is critical. In doing so, the interplay of legal and technical patent issues must be considered from the economic dimension.

3.4.2
Patenting an "Invention in Progress"

The particular problems inventors face are: when to first file an application? How to protect additional technology developed after the first filing? How to align the R&D process with the legal and financial restrictions imposed by law and the scarcity of resources?

Such "strategy" bridges the gap between the short-term tactics on the single-application level and the longer-term considerations of whether to licence out, use within an existing organisation or to start an independent venture around a portfolio.

When to File First

The first application should be filed as early as possible to minimise the risk of the invention being pre-empted by either a publication or an earlier patent. Even a delay of a single day may give the entire invention to a competitor.

The task of writing the specification aside, an application can be filed as soon as the invention has been sufficiently "reduced to practice", a criterion from US patent law which is widely used. As discussed previously, the requirements of sufficient disclosure vary between jurisdictions, but a patent attorney will be able to advise on the right time to file a first application. As a rule of thumb, better early than late: there is no remedy against being pre-empted by a competitor.

The underlying reasoning here is that the risk of losing the ability to protect the invention, however small, is not worth any advantage conferred by delaying a first application. The reader who is familiar with the idea of balancing risk and expected result, which permeates most chapters of this book, is invited to return to the issue later in this chapter. There may be situations where indeed the risk of filing late can be balanced by a particular constellation in circumstance. As a generalisation, however, filing early and adapting the later strategy to the day of filing seems good advice.

Claiming Priority under the Paris Convention

Once an application is filed, it cannot be expanded by new material. If upon further research, the invention is no longer considered complete, the applicant can file a new and expanded application. Such later application can be filed within twelve months of the filing of the first one, and this younger application can claim the "priority" of the older one.

Such claiming of priority has two aspects, regulated by the Paris Convention:
- The later application claiming priority does not face the content of the earlier (the priority of which is claimed) as offending state of the art.
- If any publication discloses the content of the earlier application, after the priority date but before the filing date of the later application, this disclosure is not held against the later application. This protection however only extends to the matter disclosed in the first application.

The simplest form of protecting an evolving technology is to file a first priority application at home. Once a filing date is established for that initial filing, the applicant has twelve months to file another application that claims the priority of the first one. That second application may contain newer, additional inventive elements, as long as the requirement of unity (one single inventive principle for all claims of the application) is respected.

In order to enjoy the benefit of priority, any embodiment of the invention claimed in the younger application needs to have been disclosed in its entirety in the priority application. At least in the European realm, case law has set strict limits to the possibility of claiming priority. The material and claims that are introduced only into the later application will not enjoy the priority of the filing date of the first priority application, but are given their own priority date.

The advantage of including additional elements in one application, rather than filing a new, independent application, is a reduction of costs. Also, there may be an issue regarding the non-obviousness if the element introduced later does not constitute an invention on its own.

Especially in technologically competitive areas, the applicant will want to leave newly developed inventive elements unprotected for as short a time as possible, so as not to expose them to being published or patented by competitors. This may require filing applications including the novel elements at each step of the inventive process. Since an application can claim more than one priority, all these additional applications could give rise to one final application claiming the priority of each element-related application.

Care has to be taken, however, that the date of the initial filing determines the expiry of the twelve months priority period. Additional applications may be filed and their priority may also be claimed, but the time from the first to the "final" application is twelve months. An additional element developed, for example, fifteen months after the initial filing cannot be added to the invention by filing a new application and claiming priority of the first application.

Box 6
Example Priorities

The following example illustrates the use of priority to protect an evolving invention, using the now-familiar steam cooker.

A first filing, Application A, by applicant Alpha discloses only the steam cooker, and is filed on January 1st, 00. The same applicant then files an additional application B disclosing a safety valve, claiming priority of the A application, on April 1st of the same year. Another application C disclosing a fastening mechanism for the lid is filed on Oct. 1st, in which the priorities of A and B are claimed.

All elements of the invention are filed on January 1st, 01, in a follow-up PCT application claiming the priorities of the earlier applications A, B and C. The individual elements contained in the PCT application, the steam cooker principle, the valve and the fastening mechanism thus enjoy the priorities of January, April and October, respectively. A competitor Omega filing a patent X on a steam cooker with a safety valve on May 2nd 00 would be coming late in comparison to both elements: the steam cooker and the valve.

Had Omega filed a patent Y describing the steam cooker and valve on February 2nd, he would not receive a patent on the steam cooker technology, but would have an earlier priority with respect to the valve element. The patent office would only grant claims to the valve technology to Omega, and Alpha would be granted a patent only on the base technology and the fastening mechanism. The initial applicant would thus be dependent on the competitor in the valve area, but enjoy protection of the steam cooker and the fastening mechanism.

If applicant Alpha filed an application D on yet another additional element, a cooking insert to separate cooking goods from the water inside the steam cooker, on April 1ˢᵗ of year 01, Alpha could not claim the priority of the original A application, which is now fifteen months old. Alpha would have to file another application. The original applications A, B and C would be prior art to this application D. Whether they are prior art only for determining novelty or also for non-obviousness, depends on the jurisdiction.

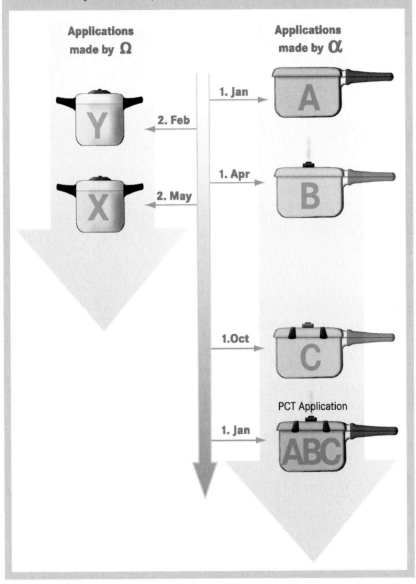

Abandoning Applications

The applicant in the above example had to file a new application to protect the ele-ments added in application D, since more than 12 months had passed since the initial A Application.

- The applicant may prefer to avoid this second, independent filing due to the cost of developing a new and independent patent fami-ly, and conflicts of obviousness or inventive step. The new ele-ments, may not, for example, constitute a sufficiently inventive to justify a new patent.

To incorporate application D into the existing patent family, the applicant may elect to abandon all previous applications and to file an application D without ben-efit of priority. "Abandoning" the application entails written notification of the pat-ent office, that the applicant does not wish to pursue any further the application, and dropping any claims to priority from that application. No rights to the priority may remain in force.

The obvious danger in this strategy is that by abandoning the previous applica-tion, the applicant risks that similar technology was made public between the time of first filing and the second filing. Even exhaustive searches do not protect against the possibility that such a publication may exist unnoticed and later emerge in the examination procedure. At any rate, remember that at the time of filing the applicant will not be aware of any technology that has been filed for pat-ent protection in the previous 18 months. While this risk always exists, it is com-pounded if the filing process is repeated again more than 12 months after the ini-tial filing.

3.4.3
Patent Deadlines Driving Development

If it is accepted that few mechanisms, if any, apart from the use of the twelve-month priority period, exist to adapt the mechanism of patent protection to the pace of invention, the consequence is that the pace of invention must be matched to the mechanics of patenting.

Three deadlines are of utmost importance in this respect.

- The first is the twelve month priority period, in which additional elements may be added to what was disclosed in the initial appli-cation.
- The second important event defining patenting of an ongoing inventive process is the publication of the initially filed applica-tion 18-months after the application date. With this publication, any subsequent filing will face the content of the first application as "state of the art", and in most jurisdictions will be an important benchmark for the inventive step of the second application.
- The third important deadline is the 30-month period of the PCT II phase. Before expiry of that phase, the applicant has to "natio-

nalize" an eventual PCT application before the national (or regional, as in the case of the EPO) offices. In most countries this
requires the applicant to hire a patent representative, to have the
PCT application translated into the official language of the respective office. This process costs between 5 and 10 thousand € per
country.

In most cases, such heavy spending can only be justified by realistic expectation
of substantial profits. For such expectations to be realistic a great deal of intelli-
gence needs to have been gathered. The invention, including the commercial
aspects such as marketing plans, pricing, manufacture and regulatory and legal
aspects need to be sufficiently clear so as to be able to make informed and rational
decisions.

Just how clear the commercial prospects of an invention must be to go beyond
the 30-month deadline will depend on the size of the eventual market for the
product. Billion-Euro pharmaceutical blockbuster hopefuls certainly will have a
higher tolerance to risk at this stage than short-lived consumer goods with low
margins.

The acquisition of the necessary development results and business intelli-
gence is itself a resource-consuming venture, and financing this activity in itself
depends on an assessment of risk and reward. In this the development and
patenting game turns into a reiterative and ongoing assessment of opportunity
and risk.

While this is probably true, or should be, for almost any technical or indeed
commercial activity, it cannot be overstated that here, the existence of deadlines
imposes very strict rules on the management of this process. While outside the
patent-driven technology world, assessments of risk and opportunities may be tak-
en with some freedom as to the exact time when they are taken (because often,
the nature of scientific and technical development defies predefined timelines),
the patent timelines are unyielding. Decisions taken with less than optimal information tend to be less than optimal, and hence, lead to losses.

3.5
Conflict

Patents are tools for conflict and a willingness to use the patent this way is its *rai-
son d'etre*. For the same reason, a valuable patent is a target for challenge. Conflict
can affect the owner of a patent in different forms:

1. The owner's patent is challenged during proceedings or after
   granting in the opposition phase or revocation procedure.
2. The patent owner is dependent on other patents and wishes
   to remove these.
3. The invention protected by the patent is used by third parties
   without authorisation of the patent owner (infringement).

All three situations allow the patent owner or the opposing party to engage in extended litigation. The first and second scenarios share legal tools, whilst the third scenario necessitates a different set of legal measures.

The arguments employed during litigation inevitably follow a preset script: On one side the patent owner, defending the validity of the patent, and in case of an infringement proceeding, affirming that the allegedly infringing commercial use falls under the scope of the patent. On the other side the attacker or alleged infringer, attacking the validity of the patent and contesting that the commercial use does not fall under the scope of the patent's claims. Often the accusation of infringement prompts the alleged infringer to attack the patent in question, so that both legal processes are able to run in parallel.

The outcome of litigation is, as ever, dependent on circumstances. Procedures and legal practice differs between countries, and since conflict is immensely multifactorial, an in-depth treatment of the topic would go beyond the scope of this book. In the event of conflict, the affected party will certainly need to seek counsel from a competent attorney.

3.5.1
Opposition

Many but not all jurisdictions provide for a formal period after the examination process, in which any third party can present arguments against the granting of a particular patent. Opposition against a European Patent requires only one process before the EPO. Presented arguments are restricted to those of patentability; particularly of novelty, non-obviousness and sufficient disclosure.

If the patent office agrees with the applicant, the patent is upheld without modification in its initial form. A finding for the opposing party may require the claims of the patent to be resubmitted with narrowed scope, or in extreme cases, the patent may not be granted at all.

An examined patent may not come into force until the opposition procedure has been formally concluded. If a patent has been granted and the opposition period has expired, or the patent has been granted after the opposition procedure, the patent is in force. Only non-payment of maintenance fees, wilful abandonment by the applicant, or successful challenge by a revocation process will now affect its existence until expiry of the 20-year term.

3.5.2
Revocation

Opposition proceedings are a regulative part of the patent granting activity, and thus allow any interested party to oppose a patent. Revocation is a last recourse and is often only available to parties that are affected by the granted patent. It is the weapon of choice against granted and effective patents.

The arguments that can be brought forward during revocation resemble those in the opposition process, although depending on jurisdiction, there may be a restriction to only the most material of arguments such as novelty and non-obviousness. As patents are a right given by individual countries, they need to be attacked through revocation on a country-by-country basis. Depending on the country, special civil or merchant courts handle these procedures.

3.5.3
Infringement

Freedom-to-Operate and Third Parties' Rights

The ability to commercially operate in a technical field is likely to be restricted by other people's patents. Inventors are well advised to establish the freedom-to-operate granted by the scope of such prior IP before embarking on research and development activities. In the worst case if no technology license can be obtained to permit the commercialisation of a patent, the investment in research is rendered worthless. Freedom-to-operate assessment follows the methodology of research into novelty and non-obviousness of an invention, described earlier in this chapter, except that it discriminates between the claim and description section of a document, and treats examined and granted patents very differently.

Generally, the user of a technology researching possible third party rights is primarily interested in the claims of examined and granted patents. Infringement of such claims can result in immediate litigation. Claims in an application, on the other hand, may be narrowed or widened during examination.

Depending on the situation, particularly the economic interest and capabilities of the inventor, two directions can be followed: the offending patent can be attacked or licensed. In order to instruct a lawyer, or to negotiate a license, detailed research into the validity or possible weaknesses of the patent should be undertaken. The cost and risk of offensive measures such as revocation or opposition, and cooperative strategies can then be compared. This research should not stop at performing a novelty and non-obviousness search; offices may allow inspection of the patent files revealing arguments used by applicants in defence of their application, and giving important hints regarding weaknesses of the patent.

If a patent is to be attacked, experienced attorneys with a history of successful litigation need to be hired. The enormous cost of these procedures is the reason why relatively few patents are attacked.

Infringement by Third Parties

If the owner of a patent detects the commercial use of the invention without licence, they have the right to sue the infringer in the country where the illegal activity is performed. Procedures vary between jurisdictions, but a lawyer is universally recommended. Evidence of the infringing action should be obtained in admissible form and format.

Before pursuing this path, however, a few questions need to be asked. The alleged infringer will in all likelihood analyse the patent in great depth. If issues of ownership, novelty, non-obviousness or disclosure surround the patent, litigation may ultimately result not in enforcement of the patent, but in its elimination. Any weak point of the patent will be discovered if the economic stakes are sufficiently high, and business literature is full of such tales. The difficulty of enforcing weak patents reinforces the need for a thorough and diligent drafting and prosecution process, eliminating as many weaknesses of the patent as possible.

In most cases, however, patents are a secondary right which frame and protect the commercial interests of the applicant and the competition. Whereas thinking about patents and law inevitably invokes prohibition and penalty, the currency of commerce is negotiation and settlement. The latter should always be considered as an alternative to the cost and risk of litigation.

Settlement

Litigation is always expensive, particularly with respect to patents. Technical specialists will be needed to give opinion on matters that legal experts find hard to judge. Moreover, prolonged litigation is accompanied by uncertainty about the future economic and legal framework of the affected business, translating into cost and shareholder doubt. To a start-up company in which continued financing depends upon an undisputed IP portfolio and a freedom to operate, such uncertainty can threaten the continued existence of the company.

Litigation and opportunity costs are the main reason why parties in a patent dispute tend to settle. The settlement may not always reflect the respective legal positions of the parties, but rather their economical strength. Settlements may entail a licence, often a cross-licence by which two parties give each other rights to their respective IP. A drastic but dramatic settlement is the acquisition of one party by the other. Issues surrounding settlement resemble those of any other licence agreement, reviewed in detail in Chapter 6.

3.6
Business Brief

Drafting a solid patent application requires the detailed collation of the material that describes the invention. A thorough search of the prior art needs to be performed to assess the opportunities of patenting and to formulate claims that have a realistic chance of being granted.

It is highly advisable to hire an experienced attorney to draft and prosecute the application. Many jurisdictions require that non-resident applicants employ a professional representative familiar with the local legal system. Applicants should apply care to structure the client-attorney relationship according to need and expectation.

The application may be filed by various means of communication. A schedule of fees is in place for most steps in the application, prosecution, issuing and maintenance process. In the event of extreme urgency, emergency filings can be submitted that can be drafted in very little time to ensure a certain priority date.

Filings will be published 18 months after the priority date. Applicants may request early publishing to put the invention on record as an impediment to competitive patents, or to enforce the preliminary protection conferred by a published application.

Filings may, on the other hand, be abandoned to avoid publication of the application. Care needs to be taken to abandon and inhibit the publication of all related applications worldwide.

The initial filing may later be changed during examination; in particular, claims may be added or changed. No substantive matter however can be added with the same priority.

Examined patents may be subject to opposition before becoming effective. If the patent is opposed, claims may be changed or the entire patent may not be granted. Once a patent is issued, it can only be attacked in the revocation process. Such attacks are rare, due to the significant cost associated with the proceedings.

Litigation on patent issues also involves substantial cost and may result in protracted periods of commercial uncertainty. In many cases, settlement between parties of a substantiated patent dispute will be a solution beneficial to both parties involved.

4
Ownership

Rolf Sander

4.1
The Rights of the Inventor

In general, intellectual property rights may be divided into the personal right to be acknowledged as the creator of the intellectual property, and the commercial right to exploit economically the fruits of this creativity. Creation itself may take many forms: development of a technical invention, computer programming, design of a chair, authorship or translation of a book. The developer of an improved video camera, for example, has the right to be named as the inventor in the patent application that derives from the invention. Whether the same inventor has a right to exploit this invention commercially will depend on circumstances such as whether the invention was made in partnership with another inventor or during the course of employment. This chapter addresses these questions, the answers to which differ significantly from country to country. Readers are advised to seek advice tailored to their specific situation and geography.

From a legal point of view, the inventor cannot transfer this personal right, for example, to a friend to enhance their reputation as an inventor. It is also impossible to nominate a person who has contributed nothing to the invention as a joint inventor. Indeed the personal rights to intellectual property are generally not transferable, and this chapter only makes reference to rights of exploitation.

These commercial rights comprise, for example, the right to license a patent or the right to sue someone for infringing a patent, a registered design or utility model. These exploitation rights have a large economical impact, and accordingly, they may be transferred to any natural or legal person. A "natural" person is a human being, whereas a "legal" person is a legally registered entity such as a corporation, university or foundation.

In essence the commercial rights to intellectual property belong to its creator. Creators are natural persons, and in most jurisdictions a legal person like a company, which acts through authorised natural persons, may not itself be a creator. Nevertheless, companies, as employers, may have the right to claim ownership of intellectual property created by their employees. This chapter discusses employee invention ownership in depth.

Intellectual Property Management. Claas Junghans, Adam Levy
Copyright © 2006 WILEY-VCH Verlag GmbH & Co. KGaA, Weinheim

4.1.1
What is an Applicant?

A basic requirement for most common intellectual property rights is a formal application to the proper national or international authority. A proper national authority may be, for example, the US-Patent and Trademark Office or the Korean Intellectual Property Office. International authorities, sometimes called regional offices include the European Patent Office and the World Intellectual Property Office. Copyrights do not require a formal request, and they arise from the act of creating the copyright. A copyright of a computer program arises from listing the source code.

In the formal application the name and address of the person who files the request must be supplied. This person, legal or natural, or group of legal or natural persons, is termed the applicant of the requested intellectual property. At least in the countries of the European Union, the applicant is deemed to be entitled to exercise the right to intellectual property, and achieves a formal legal position by applying for a patent, regardless of the underlying right to apply.

4.1.2
Applicants in the United States of America

The United States differs from European and other patent territories in its treatment of inventors and applicants. Only the inventor is entitled to apply for a United States patent, and initially no distinction is made between inventors and applicants. Only after the filing of the application by the inventor, may the application be assigned by the inventor to a third person. This assignment must be executed by the inventor, and filed with the US Patent and Trademark Office. This different treatment of inventors and applicants in the US is reflected in the PCT application process; to be eligible for a US patent inventors must sign the application as "applicants for the United States of America only".

4.1.3
Joint Applicants

Many inventions are made by several inventors, and in such cases the right to the invention jointly belongs to the inventors. As a consequence, they can apply for a patent together, becoming joint applicants. Several questions emerge here: how far can one of the joint applicants act independently of the other applicants? To what extent can one applicant bind the other applicants by force of the joint application or patent? Can each applicant sell or transfer their share of the joint application to a third party? What is the joint patent application process?

As elsewhere in the treatment of ownership issues, the answer to these questions depends greatly upon the country involved. The nature of joint ownership may give rise to very different scenarios, and competent advice is of utmost importance in assessing the consequences of any specific situation. In certain jurisdictions, notably the USA, joint applicants or patent owners may each independently grant licences to the invention to third parties. This means that even in the event of an unsettled dispute between applicants, both are free to commercialize their patent, though they will be unable to offer an exclusive licence. In other territories on the other hand, civil law statues stipulate that neither joint applicant can give a licence to a third party without the consent of the other.

It is easy to foresee the potential for disagreement between co-inventors, and conflict-free joint ownership necessitates a shared view of the rights and obligations of each inventor, as illustrated by the following example. What happens, for example, when one inventor wants the invention to remain secret? What happens if one partner wants to withdraw the patent application? What happens when partners do not equally share the costs of patenting, or when either or both inventors have a duty to transfer ownership to an employer? Patent law does not provide resolution to all of these issues, and any dispute must be resolved ahead of the deadlines prescribed by the patent process. Given this, it is highly recommended to agree the principles by which co-invention and joint-ownership will operate and to formalise relationships, however cordial, in advance of patent application, and ideally before commencing the inventive process.

Box 7
Example of joint ownership

Mr. Green and Ms. Red have developed an improved flat screen display. Before they started this joint development they did not formally agree their rights and obligations. Green believes that the development should remain a secret until further work is completed, whilst Red, wary of competition, is keen to patent the invention as quickly as possible. In order to keep the peace, Green agrees to jointly file a priority patent application in their native Turkey. The Turkish Patent Office sends its search report 10 months later to the joint inventors. In order to claim the priority of the Turkish patent application, Green wants to file a patent application in France, Japan and the United States of America. Red wants to file patents in the United Kingdom and Sweden. They agree to act as joint applicants in Japan and the United States, where Green pays the fees. They furthermore agree to file an application with the European Patent Office. According to the European Patent Convention a patent application may be filed either by joint applicants or by applicants nominating different contracting states, and Green acts as the applicant in France, Red as the applicant in the UK. The invention is a great commercial success in the USA, but Green refuses to share revenues, claiming that as he paid for the patent, he is entitled to the revenues. Meanwhile Red is exporting the invention from France to the UK and denying Green European revenues. Red decides to assign her Japanese rights to a Japanese company, which incorporates the invention into one of its own products. Meanwhile Green's employer has issued a civil action against Green, claiming ownership of the invention.

4.2
Disputed Ownership

Dispute among inventors and applicants as to the inventorship and ownership of an invention is not uncommon. Outright misappropriation or theft is an extreme case, whilst disputes arising from collaboration between inventors is more common, particularly when these relationships are poorly defined, inventors are employed by different organisations, or when one inventor is less involved in the patent, usually until its economic value is demonstrated.

The resolution of these disputes depends on the case, the geography and the circumstances, and if involved in such a case, consultation with a competent attorney is highly recommended. Careful agreement of objectives, expectations, relationships and roles, formalised before commencing the inventive process is time well-spent in avoiding such situations.

Indeed, even in the case of theft of an invention, the patent process can produce a few surprises. To take the example of an invention that is stolen by an acquaintance after an informal conversation, and subsequently filed with the EPO; although the applicant did not make the invention, and is therefore not entitled to apply, he makes the statement that the commercial right to the invention has been transferred to him by the inventor. Investigation of the applicants claim to have a right to the invention is not part of the EPO proceedings, and the now-former acquaintance is considered to be the applicant.

The possibilities to rectify this situation differ from country to country. In this example, the applicant is not entitled to the grant of a European patent, because neither is he the inventor, nor does an assignment exist between the inventor and the applicant. The inventor remains the entitled owner of the invention, and may sue the applicant to surrender the formal position. The European Patent Convention dictates that such claims are not regulated by the European Patent Office, however, but are brought before the "Proper national authorities"; the national civil courts of the nation in which the untruthful applicant lives. The European Protocol on Recognition ensures that the decision of this local court is also accepted by most contracting states of the European Patent Convention.

The decision from the national authority is presented to the European Patent Office, which offers a choice of three alternatives as to how to proceed. The inventor may prosecute the application, continuing where the former applicant left off, file a new application in respect of the same invention, or request that the application be rejected in its entirety.

4.2.1
Interference Procedure in the United States of America

Aside from the differences in treatment of inventors and applicants, US law also differs in its treatment of the ownership of identical inventions that have been independently developed. European and most other systems give a patent to the inventor who first applies for an invention. In the US the right to the patent is reserved for the person who first made the invention. Hence, over and above the issue of outright theft, disputed inventorship priority may arise. Such problems are addressed in "interference" proceedings.

The purpose of the interference procedure in the United States is to determine the date of invention, as opposed to the filing date of the application. An inventor, although filing an application which overlaps with a preceding patent, can claim an earlier invention date and therefore establish an earlier patent right. In the interference procedure the inventor must prove an inventive activity before the established priority date.

In the US an inventive act comprises two different steps; conception and reduction to practice. Conception is a mental act, and may be described as the formation in the inventors mind of a definite and permanent idea of the complete and operative invention as it is thereafter to be applied in practice. Reduction to practice is the realization of the complete invention in a physical form. An invention may be reduced to practice by actually embodying the invention of the patent into practical form by building a working model or, if the invention is related to a method, by practicing the process. This is called "actual" reduction to practice. The invention may also be filed as a patent application, and this is termed "constructive" reduction to practice.

In determining priority of invention not only are the respective dates of conception and reduction to practice considered, but also the diligence of the inventors in reducing the invention to practice. An inventor who is the first to conceive of an invention but is not first to reduce the invention to practice, may nevertheless be considered to be the "inventor" if he or she can demonstrate diligence towards this goal. Diligence may be defined as a reasonable effort directed towards the embodiment of an invention in physical form or towards a patent application.

The regulations of the interference procedure before the USPTO are evidently complex and can not be given in detail here. However, it should be noted that proving an earlier date of conception, reduction to practice or proving diligence requires evidence in the form of written records documenting experiments or the development of the invention, or confirmation by an independent witness. Interference proceedings are more than an academic interest for inventors outside of the US, since non-US applicants registering for US patent protection may be faced with claims of older priority. An inventor who plans to patent in the US is well advised to record any act of invention thoroughly in order to prepare for such a dispute.

4.3
Employee or Service Inventions

Due to the specialization of technology and the need for sophisticated equipment, many inventions are now made by the research teams of established companies and the economic significance of inventions made by private inventors in their attics and sheds has diminished. There is therefore the need for a clear set of principles to establish to whom employee inventions belong. In the field of employee or service inventions these principles are laid down by the sometimes-conflicting regulations of intellectual property and industrial law.

For example, according to the principle of inventorship the invention belongs to the inventor. This conflicts with the principle of industrial law, according to which the work belong to the employer. In order to uphold both principles, most jurisdictions stick to the principle of inventorship by stipulating that even a service invention originally belongs to the employed inventor, but that the inventor must transfer the patent rights to the employer. This transfer might be regulated in advance by, for example, a contract of employment. In general however it is difficult to predict the economic impact of an invention, and employees are economically and socially dependent on their employer. Given this asymmetry of power, employers may take advantage of employees, and some countries do not therefore allow such advance transfers of IP rights.

In general, several questions arise with regard to service inventions. At what point does a collaboration constitute employment. What happens if the employer does not believe the invention is patentable and refuses to file it? Is the employer working in a research and development role and therefore expected to invent? Has the employer supported the inventor by providing knowledge, resources or direction? As with many areas of patent law in general, regulations regarding service inventions across jurisdictions, as discussed below on a country-by-country basis.

4.3.1
Germany

The German Law on Employee Inventions distinguishes between tied and free inventions. Tied service inventions are those made during the term of employment, regardless of whether the invention was made during working hours, the weekend or even on vacation. A tied invention must however, have resulted from an employee's duties within the company, or be based on the experience or activities of the company. The employee's duties may be described in the labour contract or other work regulation documents.

Initially all inventions belongs to the inventor, who is obliged to notify the employer about a tied service invention by making a special written notice. In the subsequent four-month period the employer may take ownership of the inventive rights by a written declaration to the inventor, making a choice between an "unlimited" and a "limited" claim. In the case of an unlimited claim the employer acquires ownership of all rights to the tied service invention granting the employee reasonable compensation. If the employer declares a limited claim, it has a non-exclusive right to using the invention, and the employee has a claim to compensation only when the employer uses the invention. If the employer makes no declaration within the four-month period or releases the invention, the invention is treated as a free invention, and the right to exploit the invention belongs to the employee. For a tied service invention the employer must file a national patent or utility model application unless the employee agrees that no application should be filed. In declaring an unlimited claim the employer is also granted the right to file the invention in countries other than Germany. The employee must be given timely notice of countries in which the employer does not want to file, and must be allowed to acquire protection in these countries. When the employer wants to abandon a patent or patent application based on a service invention before fully compensating the inventor, the employee must be informed, and offered all rights. The employer may reserve a non-exclusive right.

Remuneration for a service invention is based on the revenue from products in which the invention is used, adjusted according to guidelines laid down by the Minister of Labour. This adjustment reflects the contribution of the invention to the overall revenue of a product, the involvement of the employee in making the invention, and the position of the employee within the company. The closer the invention to his duties, or the higher the employee within the company, the lower the factor. Usually the employee's contributing factor is about 15% and typical royalty rates lie between 0.5–5% in the field of electronics, 0.33–10% in the machinery field, 2–5% in chemistry, and 2–10% in pharmacy.

In the case of a free invention made in the course of employment, the employee must inform the employer and provide sufficient information to support the claim that the invention is free. The employer has a three-month period in which to contest ownership of the invention. Before exploiting a free invention that falls within the employer's activities an employee must offer the employer a non-exclusive license under reasonable conditions. License fees for free inventions are four to five times greater than the compensation fees for tied inventions.

4.3.2
United Kingdom

In the United Kingdom the regulations regarding employee or service inventions declare that a service invention belongs to the employer, if

- the invention was made in the course of the employee's normal duties, or
- in the course of duties falling outside normal duties, but specifically assigned to the employee, and
- the circumstances in either case were such that an invention might reasonably be expected to result from the performance of these duties, or
- the invention was made in the course of the employee's duties under a special obligation to further the interests of the employer because of the nature of the duties. The duties of the employee may be fixed in the employment contract.

The employee may claim reasonable compensation if a patent based on the employees invention is granted and the employer receives a benefit from the patent. The gain the employer receives from the patent, however, has to be distinguished from the benefit from the invention alone. Benefits resulting only from the patent are usually hard to identify unless the patent is licensed or sold to a third party, and in practice, it is quite common that compensation is subject to free negotiation.

4.3.3
France

In France employees must inform employers of inventions made during the course of employment, and must classify the invention according to the three categories below. The employer has a two-month period in which to contest this classification.

- The invention falls within the scope of the inventor's duties or tasks, which are defined in the employment contract.
- The invention does not fall within the scope of the inventor's duties; however, the invention is related to the employer's business, is based on the employer's knowledge, or the employee used the employers resources.
- The invention falls outside of the scope of the employee's duties and of the employer's business.

If the invention falls within the inventor's duties, the invention belongs to the employer, but the employee is entitled to additional remuneration. If the invention falls within the second category it belongs to the employee, but within a four-month period following the receipt of the invention report the employer may claim all, or a part, of the commercial rights to the invention for a fair price. The terms and conditions of additional remuneration and "fair prices" are not regulated by law, but by collective agreements or guidelines, which differ according to the nature of the business. If the invention is classified according to the third category the invention belongs in its entirety to the employee.

4.3.4
Spain

According to Spanish Patent Law, inventions made by an employee during the term of contracted work with a company, which result from research that is explicitly or implicitly the object of the contract, belong to the employer. The employee-inventor has no claim to additional remuneration except where the personal contribution to the invention and its importance obviously go beyond the explicit or implicit terms of the contract. In general, this means that the employee has no claim to additional remuneration if the invention falls within the scope of normal duties.

When an employee makes an invention that is not the result of research defined in the labour contract, the invention belongs to the employee. However, if the invention is related to the employee's professional activity or was made using the knowledge or resources of the company, the employer has the right to claim ownership of the invention or to reserve a right to its use. In this case the employee has the right to reasonable remuneration fixed in relation to the invention's commercial importance and the relative contributions of the company and of the employee to the invention.

In any case, the employee-inventor must inform the employer in writing, providing sufficient information so that the employer may exercise its rights within a period of three months. Failure to fulfil this obligation leads to the loss of the rights granted to the employee under Spanish patent law. The employer and the employee must collaborate so that, for example, a patent application may be filed, and neither party is allowed to publish the invention before the filing date of the application.

4.3.5
Russia

Inventions made in the course of an employee's normal tasks or duties are regarded as employee-inventions in the Russian Federation and the employer is the initial owner under the labour contract defining the tasks and duties of the employee. The employee must inform the employer about the invention and has a claim to reasonable remuneration. If the employer does not, within four months, file a patent application, transfer the right to the patent to a third person or inform the employee that the invention is to be kept a trade secret, the employee has the right to file a patent application. The employer retains the right to use the invention, making reasonable compensation to the employee. An invention made outside the scope of an employee's duties is not considered a service invention and it belongs fully in its entirety to the employee.

4.3.6
USA

In the United States, the inventor must file the invention with the US Patent and Trademark Office, and as a result US companies are extremely diligent in defining the employment contracts that regulate assignment of inventions to the company. Employees are generally not entitled to additional remuneration.

4.3.7
Japan

According to Japanese Patent Law an invention belongs to its inventor. Indeed, whilst an employee-invention is defined as one that falls within the scope of the employer's business as part of the present or past duties of the employee, there is no statutory assignment of the employee-invention to the employer. Employee-inventions, but not other inventions, may however be assigned in advance, and Japanese employment contracts include assignment of IP rights to the employer.

In the case of an assignment or license of a patent, the employee has a claim to reasonable remuneration. The level of remuneration depends on the invention-related profit of the employer and the employee's contribution to the invention. There is no guideline or further legal definition of the terms and method of payment, and in the past, remuneration has not been in line with international levels.

Indeed, in recent years several Japanese companies have been sued by former employees for additional compensation. In the most prominent example the court decided in favour of Mr. Nakamura, the inventor of the blue light-emitting diode, which is used in video screens and coloured display devices. Mr. Nakamura initially received only 200 € for this invention and was subsequently awarded 2 million €. Given this degree of inequity, remuneration levels within Japan are understandably facing review.

4.3.8
Korea

According to the Korean Patent Act an employee-invention is an intellectual creative work of invention, conception or creation by an employee in connection with normal duties and which belongs, by its nature, to the scope of the employer's business. The employer has only a right to a non-exclusive licence to these inventions. As in Japan, however, the employer may enter into special contracts with its employees, by which the rights to employee-inventions are transferred to the company, even before they exist. Most companies located in Korea have employment contracts containing such regulations. If an employee transfers the right to obtain a patent for an invention to an employer, or grants the employer an exclusive license, the employee is entitled to reasonable compensation.

4.3.9
China

According to Chinese Patent Law, a service invention belongs to the employer. An employee or service invention is defined as one made in the course of one's duties, or in the execution of any task entrusted by the employer or made mainly by using the material or resources of the employer. Inventions meeting these criteria made within one year of resignation, retirement or change of work also belong to the employer. The employee-inventor is entitled to reasonable compensation.

4.3.10
Hungary

Patent law in Hungary distinguishes between service inventions and employee inventions. A service invention is one made by a person who, by reason of employment, is under the obligation to develop solutions in the field of the invention. An employee invention is an invention made by a person who is not under such an obligation. The exploitation rights of a service invention belong to the employer. The exploitation rights of an employee invention belong to the inventor but the employer has a right to a non-exclusive license.

The inventor must notify the employer of any invention immediately following its creation. Within 90 days the employer may claim title to the service invention, or state an intention to commercialise an employee invention. In the absence of a claim the inventor is granted exclusive ownership of both service and employee inventions.

In the case of a claimed service invention, the employer must file a patent application within a reasonable time, and must proceed with all due diligence to obtain a patent. Under the condition that the invention is kept secret and exploited as a trade secret, the employer may alternatively acknowledge the patentability of the invention. In the event of a dispute, the burden of proving that a solution was not patentable falls to the employer. If intending to withdraw a patent application based on a service invention, the employer must offer the corresponding rights to the inventor free of charge.

If a service or employee invention is used, the inventor has a right to reasonable remuneration, and no derogation by contract from this provision is permissible.

4.3.11
Czech Republic

When an invention is made as part of tasks deriving from an employment relationship, or from membership of an organisation, the right to the patent passes to the employer, unless otherwise laid down by contract.

The employee inventor must notify the employer about the invention without delay in writing, and must pass on all the necessary information and documents regarding the invention. The employer may claim the right to the patent within a period of three months. Otherwise the right reverts to the inventor. Both employer and employee must maintain the secrecy of the invention.

If the employer claims the right to the patent, the employee inventor is entitled to reasonable remuneration, based on the technical and economic importance of the invention, the material contribution of the employer to the invention, and the extent of the inventor's service obligations.

4.3.12
Poland

According to the Industrial Property Law of Poland the right to obtain a patent for an invention initially belongs to its creator. The exploitation rights of an invention made by an inventor in the course of employment duties or in the execution of any other contract belong to the employer, unless otherwise agreed. If an employer assists in the invention by an employee, it enjoys the right to exploit the invention in its own field of activity. The employee-inventor is entitled to remuneration for the employer's exploitation of an invention. If the parties fail to agree this remuneration, it is determined by reference to the profits obtained by the employer, the extent to which the inventor was assisted in making the invention, and the scope of the inventor's employment duties in making the invention. It is recommended to agree the amount and terms of this remuneration in advance, in the employment contract.

4.3.13
Sweden

The Swedish Act on Employee Inventions distinguishes between three categories of employee invention made within the field of the employer's business:

- The invention falls within the scope of the inventors duties or tasks, which are, for example, defined in the employment contract.
- The invention is related to the employer's business outside of the scope of the inventors duties, but is related to the employees employment.
- The invention falls in the scope of the employer's business but is not related to the employees employment.

If the invention falls in one of these three categories the employee must notify the employer without delay. The employer has a period of 4 months following this notification date in which to act. If the invention falls in the first category it belongs to the employer, which may take ownership of all or parts of the exploitation rights. If the invention is in the second category, the employer is entitled to a licence. In case of the final category the employee must enter into negotiations with the employer. The employee must be granted reasonable remuneration, depending on the value of the invention, the extent of the employer's right to the invention and the circumstances in which the invention was made.

4.3.14
Conclusion

Since the question of IP ownership has a great deal of overlap with civil law, there has been little attempt to harmonise ownership law through territorial treaties such as TRIPS. Indeed regulations on service inventions differ considerably, and inventors will need both to carefully consider the local laws, and to seek professional counsel in order to identify their rights and obligations, and the level of remuneration that they can expect from their invention.

5
Trademarks and Designs

Tobias Boeckh

The preceding chapters have been concerned with the Intellectual Property protection of the technical features of a product. Ideally, such protection encompasses the product, its manufacture, and its uses. Non-technical aspects can also be of great importance in protecting a commercial product. Foremost among these are trademark and design protection.

Only in the most rare of cases are products sold on the market without a name. On the contrary, a product frequently stands out by means of its skilful naming, which makes it distinguishable from other products of the same nature. The same applies to the design of a product. A lamp often does not differ from other lamps in technical terms; the design of the lamp is, however, a distinctive criterion which makes it distinguishable from other lamps. The name and the design of a product are protectable property rights.

Furthermore, products and services of all kinds are sold by companies and the designation of the company plays an important role in marketing and distinguishing products. The aim of this chapter is to provide an overview of non-technical protection rights, with particular focus on the protection of distinctive marks, designations and designs.

5.1
Protection of Distinctive Marks

"Distinctive marks" include, in general
- the trademark,
- the name of an association, company, local authority or any other person in law,
- the business designation (designation of a company, particular descriptions of a business establishment, logo and titles of works),
- geographical details of origin.

Intellectual Property Management. Claas Junghans, Adam Levy
Copyright © 2006 WILEY-VCH Verlag GmbH & Co. KGaA, Weinheim

Fundamentally, all of these rights for the protection of distinctive marks have an equal footing in law, and the time priority principle applies to establish seniority.

5.1.1
Trademark Protection

What is a Trademark and What is its Purpose?

A trademark distinguishes products or services of one company from those of another. All kinds of signs can be protected as a trademark, particularly words and names of people, illustrations, letters, figures, sound marks, 3-dimensional designs, including the shape of a product (3-dimensional trademarks) or their packaging as well as any other make-ups including colours and colour combinations. The combination of words and pictures, regardless of whether they are in colour or not, can also be protected. Examples of trademarks are:

- Combinations of letters and digits, e.g. BBC, CNN, Levi-501s, 7-ELEVEN.
- Advertising slogans or short successions of words, e.g. SLIM FAST.
- Short successions of musical notes known as jingles, e.g. Intel inside tune.
- Colours, e.g. magenta for Deutsche Telekom, blue/silver/red for Red Bull.
- Objects, e.g. the COCA COLA bottle.

The special function of a trademark is to designate the origin or maker of a product. The trademark is not to be used to indicate the product itself. For this reason, the trademark offices check whether the labelling to be registered possibly concerns names that describe the content of the product or service. The trademark may not be a synonym for the product or the service itself. The registration of the trademark "fruit" is not, for example, possible for identifying a greengrocery.

A trademark is usually in force for 10 years and can be extended, usually in increments of 10 years, for an indefinite period. Trademarks that have been in use for many years can acquire significant value. They belong to the company's property and form part of the insolvency proceedings in case of bankruptcy.

A trademark can be licensed exclusively or non-exclusively for all goods and services for which the trademark is registered, or for only a subset of these. In this, it enjoys an advantage over other rights such as company or subsidiary names that may only be transferred along with the corresponding part of the business. The complete or partial transfer is also possible. As such, the trademark is a fully licensable right indispensable for complete product production. Trademark rights are more easily enforced than patent rights. Often, an infringer will copy the name of a successful product in bringing an identical or similar product onto the market. Trademark protection is attained more easily, faster and at less cost than a patent, and many products and services can not be protected by patents at all.

The owner of a registered trademark may legally mark the trademark with the ® symbol. Using this symbol without a corresponding valid registration is considered misleading and may be sanctioned. The use of the symbols ™ or ˢᴹ is derived from US-American trademark law. The symbols indicate that the owner claims rights to a mark which is not registered. Usually, the ™ or ˢᴹ symbols are employed if the trademark is in the process of registration or the registration is planned in the near future.

National and International/Regional Trademarks

In trademark law, as in industrial property law in general, the principle of territoriality applies. A trademark is only protected in the country in which it is registered. Many firms with a regional perspective have nevertheless long-relied on the rights conferred by their firm name as a protection, but this has harmful consequences when expanding the reach of operations. Only trademark rights confer national protection, and in the case of international operations, a company name without a similar trademark registration will not give any protection at all if no local subsidiary firm is registered. This emphasizes the need to register the company name abroad as a trademark if goods or services are to be marketed under the company name internationally.

The legal principles for trademark protection are comparable in most countries, particularly in European countries. However, before filing for the registration of a trademark in the USA, legal advice should be taken since the national US trademark law differs from the European principles on many important points, particularly with regard to issues of the duration of protection, use and enforceability.

In addition to national trademarks, there are also transnational trademarks that permit simultaneous registration in a group of countries. These include European Community Trademarks (CTM), International Registrations (IR trademarks), the ARIPO and OAPI trademarks. The latter are trademarks under African regional intellectual property agreements.

Community Trademarks are registered by the OHIM, the European Union's Office for Harmonization in the Internal Market, Trade Marks and Designs, in Alicante for the entire European Union. With one registration the owner of such a trademark receives protection for labelling in all countries of the European Union. Use in one single EU country is sufficient to establish use within the entire Community, and use of the trademark in each individual country is not required. Selection of individual EU countries is not possible however, and the protection is uniform across all countries of the European Union. In the event that the trademark is rejected or is overthrown due to opposition or nullity proceedings, then the trademark protection is entirely lost. If this occurs, the Community Trademark may be converted into individual, national trademarks.

International Registrations, which are registered by the World Intellectual Property Organization (WIPO) in Geneva, afford the applicant the opportunity to extend an existent national trademark to additional countries. The Madrid Protocol, which regulates the WIPO currently has 77 member countries, including the

European Union, the United States of America, Japan, Australia and South Korea. Each country may be selected individually for protection. The prerequisite for an International Registration is the existence of a national trademark application or registration in one of these member countries. The membership of the EU provides the opportunity to extend a national trademark to the EU, or from a CTM to other member countries.

After international registration, the patent offices of the selected countries are notified by the WIPO. International Registration has the same effect as though the trademark had been filed at a national level and examination occurs in line with national laws. The countries have a time limit of 12 to 18 months for this process. The International Registration is linked to the existence of the domestic trademark for five years. Should the domestic trademark fall in this period of time, the IR trademark will also perish. Should the trademark be rejected in one of the selected countries, the IR trademark will still remain in all other selected countries. The duration of protection of the International Registration is ten years and can thereafter be extended as often as desired. Following registration, the trademark is granted full protection in each country as if it had been directly lodged there.

ARIPO (African Regional Intellectual Property Organisation) und *OAPI* (Organisation Africaine de la Propriété Intellectuelle) are African organisations for intellectual property in English and French-speaking countries of Africa in which a comparable trademark protection can be obtained for all member states.

How and Where are Trademarks Registered?

Trademarks are registered by filing application and registration in the trademark register of the national or regional trademark and patent office. Distinct from patent law, there is a uniform priority time limit of 6 months for filing application for registration. This means that within a period of 6 months after filing for registration of an initial trademark, application may be filed for registration again of the same trademark abroad while keeping the original priority. The priority time limit of 6 months also applies to the filing of application for an International Registration or a Community Trademark.

Application for international registration of a pending or registered national trademark is filed at the patent and trademark office of the home country. This patent office then passes on the application to the International Bureau of WIPO. Application fees are payable directly to the WIPO in Geneva in Swiss francs. In the case of application for registration of a Community Trademark, application may be filed either in Alicante directly or at a national office.

There is a peculiarity with regard to filing application for registration of a Community Trademark. In addition to laying claim to one or more priorities of previous applications, it is possible in the case of the Community Trademark to lay claim to the filing day of a national trademark, for which application for registration has already been filed in one of the member states of the EU, even if the filing of the previous national application dates back many years. This is termed claiming seniority.

Any individual or group of natural and legal entities is entitled to file application for the registration of a trademark. An application must contain the name of the applicants, a reproduction of the trademark and a list of goods and/or services for which the trademark is intended. As a matter of principle, all goods or services can be protected by a trademark. In the case of services, however, it must be kept in mind that these services are to be rendered for third parties and offered under the trademark. Thus it is not necessary, for example, to protect the service "advertising" insofar as this only refers to "own advertising" of one's own product.

The goods and services for which protection is being claimed are classified by the patent office in accordance with the *Nice Agreement Concerning the International Classification of Goods and Services for the Purposes of the Registration of Marks.* The official fees are calculated on the basis of the corresponding number of classes. This classification has no direct impact on the scope of protection of a trademark in any subsequent infringement action, and its main purpose is to simplify and standardise the classification of the goods/services and the calculation of fees. In most countries one single multiple-class application can be filed for protection of the most diverse goods and services even if these goods and services fall within the scope of different categories. However, once application for registration of the mark has been filed, the list of goods and services cannot be expanded, and application has to be re-filed if the list of goods is incomplete. The same applies to the mark itself: once application for registration has been filed, the mark may not be modified, for example, with regard to layout, order of letters, colours.

Examination and Registration Procedures of Trademarks
"Innovation" or "novelty" does not play a role in the registration of a trademark, and it is immaterial whether the mark already existed. This does not mean that application could be filed for registration of well-known trademarks. This rather means that the patent office does not check whether the symbol or logo has already existed in principle. The examination procedure of every authority is generally divided into three stages, namely a formal examination, a substantive examination regarding absolute protection impediments and a relative examination for possible adverse trademark rights of third parties.

During the course of the *formal examination*, the formal requirements regarding the trademark protection applied for are checked. These include, for example, application eligibility, unambiguousness of the applicant, clarity and unambiguousness of the list of goods and services as well as full payment of the filing fees.

The *examination for absolute protection impediments* addresses whether the filed identification, regardless of whether it is a word, symbol, a combination of digits or the shape of a product, is protectable at all with regard to the given goods and services. As a rule, the focus of attention of the examiner is the issue of distinctiveness and the need to keep the mark free for trade. A trademark must be distinctive and may not describe goods or contents. As a rule, expressions or illustrations based on one's own neologisms or creativity and which thus demonstrate a degree of imagination possess the necessary distinctiveness. Examination is carried out to check whether the mark may be required by competitors in the field of goods or services in question. This could be the case, for example, with units of measurements or technical terms that are commonly used in the sector concerned. In addition, the patent offices are, however also fundamentally entitled to object to the mark from other aspects, for instance if it concerns national coats of arms, symbols or emblems, quality marks or hallmarks or deceptive information or is in violation of public policy or accepted moral standards.

On the other hand, *relative protection impediments* are not to be found in the nature of the mark itself, but rather in the existence of prior identical marks or marks which could cause confusion. Two marks are regarded as capable of being confused if both the marks themselves and the protected goods/services are identical or similar. In Europe, applications are officially examined in virtually all countries to determine whether a mark with which the given mark could be confused has already been registered in one of the registers of trademarks. Should this be the case, an opposition is issued. Such oppositions can frequently be dispelled by convincing the patent office that there is no risk of confusion or by presenting a letter of consent from the proprietor of the prior mark for registration of ones own mark. Occasionally, it is also possible to dispel the concerns of the office by limiting the list of goods and services to non-conflicting goods and services.

After successful completion of the examination procedure, the mark is offered by public announcement for *opposition*. This means that any third party in possession of an older mark is entitled to raise an opposition against the registration of the mark. The mark is published in the trademark gazette of the competent patent office. The time limit for opposition, which commences upon publication, is between 1 and 3 months in many countries, though several countries do not provide for an opposition procedure.

Trademarks are protected in the country in which they are registered, and are similarly opposed on a national level, before the competent patent and trademark office. A prior mark for Great Britain can, for instance, be a prior British application or a prior Community Trademark application, or an International Registration that includes Great Britain. As a rule, it is only the proprietor of a prior mark who is actually authorised to raise an opposition. Several countries do also allow oppositions based on grounds other than prior marks. In Great Britain, for example, an opposition can also be based on the fact that the newer mark for which application has been filed conflicts with the mark of a third party that has been in use for many years. It is therefore possible to raise an opposition against a mark which is identical to an older mark but which is registered for completely different goods and services. The opposition will, however, only be successful if it can be proven that the older conflicting mark has a high degree of reputation. Other grounds that could stand in the way of a trademark being registered, such as the absence of authorisation or entitlement of the applicant to file application, are disregarded by the patent offices, and require initiation of legal proceedings.

"Notoriously well-known marks" and "agent's trademarks" provide additional grounds for opposition in most countries. A notoriously well-known mark refers to those with an extremely high degree of reputation at home, generally defined by recognition by more than 50 % of all addressed groups of market participants (consumers, dealers, competitors). Agent's trademarks refer to a trademark that was, for example, registered by a sales partner or a licensee without the consent of the actual proprietor of the mark.

The procedure before the Harmonisation Office provides for opposition based on older Community Trademarks, older national marks in an EU member state or internationally registered marks for EU member states. Moreover, an opposition before the OHIM can also be based on older well-known marks, notoriously well-known marks and older trade names that are verifiably used in a member state of the European Union. Finally, the so-called agent's trademark also constitutes grounds for opposition within the scope of the European opposition procedure.

The opposition procedure, which is open to everybody, constitutes a means of regulation for the examination practices of patent offices. Several thousand trademarks are registered annually, often after examination of absolute protection impediments only. A comparison to all prior marks is inevitably incomplete, no matter how diligently it is performed. Indeed, some countries, such as France, Italy, Switzerland and Germany do not examine the existence of prior trademark rights at all. When a comparison is performed, the patent office restricts its research to purely formal aspects regarding the similarity of a mark. A patent office cannot examine issues concerning the actual use or the entitlement to file for registration of a mark at all. The opposition procedure affords a competitor the opportunity to influence trademark registrations of third parties. This can result in a trademark not being entered or being removed from the register, despite its positive examination by the patent office.

The applicant is well advised to diligently research registered marks prior to submitting a registration. Most trademark offices offer free databases for this purpose. These however only will reveal identical word marks in most cases. There is a widely held, but false opinion that a risk of confusion of marks only exists if two marks are written identically. On the contrary, there is a risk of confusion if marks are pronounced in a similar manner, if they are phonetically identical ("Maclite" and "Mclight") or if they also have the same meaning. Some marks can also be understood as a series of marks or can be "read into" a series of marks of an outside company. For this reason, professional market research offered by patent lawyers, patent agents or professional research institutes is to be recommended. In this research, attention is not only paid to the entire identity of marks but also to their individual parts. Applicants frequently regard such research as unnecessary as it increases costs. However, opposition proceedings can take several years and involve substantial costs. In the meantime the applicant has no legal security concerning the registration of the trademark, and may indeed need to remove the mark from products in the event of an adverse opposition outcome. In this context, research costs appear relatively trivial.

Costs of Filing and Registering a Trademark

Costs for registering a trademark differ greatly. Most patent offices charge a basic fee for the filing of the application for registration of a trademark and an additional class fee. A second registration fee and class fee is also charged for subsequent transnational application, for example for a Community Trademark. Most patent offices publish filing costs on their websites, including the WIPO[1]. The following list of examples is therefore only intended as a brief overview of the anticipated costs of application for trademarks registration. The costs stated here reflect office fees and do not include fees for legal services, which can exceed these official fees. These costs vary from lawyer to lawyer and from country to country.

Table 5.1 Official fees for filing and registration of trade marks in selected countries.

Word mark in 3 classes	Official filing fee	Official registration fee	Official renewal fee
Community Trade Mark (CTM)	975 €	1100 €	2500 €
International Registration (IR for the countries BX, FR, UK, US, JP) basic registration comes from DE, transmittal fee	5597 Sfr.[2] 180 €	–	8246 Sfr.
Benelux (BX)	240 €	–	260 €
Germany (DE)	300 €	–	750 €
France (FR)	215 €	–	230 €
United Kingdom (UK)	300 £	–	300 £
United States (US)	1125 $	–	1300 $[3]
Japan (JP)	249,000 ¥	–	453,000 ¥

Different application strategies may lead to the trademark being registered in different countries, and at different overall cost. The same geographical protection can also be achieved by a number of routes, at varying cost. For example, a trademark may be registered in Europe as a CTM or an IR registration. If protection is sought in more than 7 countries, a Community Trademark is clearly less expensive, and since it automatically protects the mark in all EU member countries, it has a high intrinsic value.

1) Madrid Calculator under www.wipo.int/madrid/feecalc.
2) including 2262 Sfr. as second part fee for Japan for the publication of the mark after examination
3) application in paper form, costs approximately, including statement of use

How to Create a Trademark and a Strategy for Filing

Careful thought must be given to the design and choice of trademark prior to application. Most trademarks are word marks, consisting of words or combinations of words without any particular layout or additional picture motifs. Such marks identify and name a product.

The trademark should be chosen so as to minimize potential problems in examination. It should be innately protectable, and not be capable of being confused with the trademarks of third parties. As a rule, expressions or illustrations based on neologisms or creativity and which demonstrate imagination possess the distinctiveness to become trademarks. Marks which have been taken from common words or which contain universally established words are, however, problematic. These words are widely known and bear associations, often with the subject matter of the application, and are thus likely to receive opposition. Trademarks however are often chosen with at least some reference to the object they are to mark. Such marks are on the edge of what is allowable to register. Although the beholder of this trademark has a certain idea as to what could be meant by the trademark, he cannot specify exactly what it is in concrete terms. Such trademarks work well in practice but receive official scrutiny to ensure that the term does not describe the content of the product or service. Such brand names that are borderline in terms of protectability are often given a logo so that combined trademarks (word and picture) are created. The picture element may suppress official opposition as marks are evaluated in the manner in which the application for registration is filed, and the office may not dissect the trademark or break it down into its constituent parts. If protectability is in doubt, it is sometimes recommended that application be filed for the registration of two trademarks, namely a word trademark and a combined mark consisting of words and pictures. Generally speaking, the combined trademark is more quickly registered, but if the word mark subsequently follows, this is of greater value in practice.

From a practical point of view it is important that the trademark registration addresses the intended use. Trademarks are subject to changing times and practices, including for example developments in layout, design and presentation. This problem rarely arises in the case of word-only trademarks, as such trademarks fundamentally protect any method of presentation, such as changes in font or character, as long as the word is recognisable. If the design of a combined trademark is changed, on the other hand, due to changes in advertising, the picture trademark can change substantially in its identifying constituent parts. Should this be the case, then application for registration of new trademark should be filed for the modified design.

Advertising agencies and graphic designers can assist in design of a trademark, but may pay limited attention to the fundamental issue of registration. For this, it is advised that applicants seek the opinion of patent lawyers or agents prior to filing application. Individual applicants or companies on a tight budget, may elect to file an application, without this expense, and wait for a reaction from the trademark office.

Application should be filed for trademark registrations in the countries in which the mark will be used. If a company operates in several countries, or markets its products through sales partners in other countries, then consideration should be given to an international trademark. Often a twin-track application procedure is advisable, filing application for both national and international trademarks. This usually leads to swift registration of the national trademark and then, subsequent extension to individual countries. Direct international filings can be protracted, and applicants run the risk that the entire trademark is lost in opposition. It is well advised to seek professional counsel if an application is of particular importance, or involves international extension.

When selecting the trademark, it should also be noted that the name itself and its meaning may not create the impression of describing the content of the goods or services in any language of the European Union. As part of its examination regarding absolute protection impediments, the Harmonisation Office will check whether a particular meaning happens to be added to the term, for example, in Spanish, Portuguese or Swedish. Should this be the case and the trademark merely describes the content in Sweden, for example, this would result in the rejection of the entire trademark.

5.1.2
Internet Domains/e-Commerce

In the broadest sense, all marking rights serve the purpose of distinguishing products and services. Such marks may be trademarks, company names, natural names and indeed, Internet domain names. These domain names are increasing in commercial importance. Generally speaking, not every Internet domain name can be a trademark, due to the absence of distinctiveness, but every trademark can be an Internet domain name. If a domain name is distinctive, meets the other requirements of a trademark, and is not registered by third parties as a trademark or used in any other manner in business transactions, an application for registration of the domain name trademark is recommended. Conversely, there is little point in choosing an Internet domain name that has already been applied for, or registered by third parties, or that is used elsewhere in business dealings for identical or similar products and services.

Registration of an Internet domain name is simple, fast and inexpensive. In principle, Internet domain names are registered according to time priority and without verification of industrial property rights. For a successful trademark protection strategy it is therefore extremely advisable to register the Internet domain name that corresponds with the trademark at an early stage, even before filing application for registration of the trademark. Although it is certainly possible to have an Internet domain cancelled when it has been maliciously registered as a trademark by third parties, this can usually only be done through costly court proceedings. Configurations of the mark should be registered to ensure broad protection, although the geographic designation of the name (e.g. .uk, .fr, .de, .org, .com, .biz, .net) is not relevant. Domains should be reserved, where applicable, for e-commerce marketing of the product, though it should be remembered that the rights arising from a trademark are further-reaching than those from an Internet domain.

5.1.3
Trade Names, Company Names and Titles

In several countries unregistered trademarks, used in magazines, books and guides or similarly published, are protected by common trademark and trade law, and have the same rights as registered trademarks. Similarly to be protected as a Trade name, it is sufficient that the name is used for business purposes. Moreover, if business is conducted under a personal or natural name, the name achieves economic relevance as a Trade name. As a consequence, persons doing their business under their natural name often have the same rights as they would have on the basis of a registered name, trade name or trademark.

Unregistered titles used as titles for works are also protected by copyright. A copyright, designated by ©, is a form of intellectual property that grants authors and artists the exclusive right to the reproduction, derivation, distribution, performance and display of their original works, including literary, artistic, dramatic and musical works and computer programs. Copyright itself does not depend on official procedures, and a work is considered protected by copyright as soon as it exists. However, a title used for a book, magazine, music compact disk, computer software program, is a right similar to a registered trademark. The most important thing is that the title must be in use. Many countries have a National Copyright Office and some laws allow for registration of works for the purposes of, for example, identifying and distinguishing titles of works.

5.1.4
Appellations of Origin

A protected appellation of origin is granted to products that are produced, processed and prepared within a specific geographic region and according to a recognised and controlled method. The European Union provides such products with logos to increase their recognition whilst guaranteeing authenticity. Protected appellations of origin are generally granted to exclusive products of high quality.

5.1.5
Enforcement of Rights

Large sums of money are invested in the design and development of trademarks, in launching and promoting product names, trademarks and brands. Unauthorised use of such marks results in a loss of business, goodwill and brand identity. It is only through the enforcement of the rights arising from registered or unregistered marks that this investment is protected.

In order to enforce unregistered rights, the court must be convinced that the mark is associated in the public mind with a product or service, and that the infringer's goods have been mistaken for these. If a mark is registered, enforcement is more stratighforward. The owner may sue for infringement under national trademark law, by demonstrating that the infringer has used a mark which is the same as, or similar to, the registered mark on goods or services which are the same, or similar to, the goods or services for which the mark is registered. In certain circumstances the deliberate use of a registered mark on goods may be classed as counterfeiting. This is a criminal offence, and criminal proceedings may be initiated under trademark law. In general terms, the owner of a trademark right is entitled to forbearance and compensation for damages from the infringing party. Legal action is expensive, especially in the field of intellectual property. That should be reason enough to clarify the trademark situation in advance, and to conduct extensive research prior to registration.

5.2
Designs

5.2.1
What is a Design?

Design protection evolved from copyright law to afford artists protection from reproduction of their work, such as industrial or handicraft products. Design protection does not relate to the artistic design of a product, but primarily to how it is shaped. Nowadays, this is interpreted as the outward appearance of a product or a part thereof, which results from, in particular, the characteristics of the lines, contours, colours, shape, surface structure and the materials used to manufacture the product and its ornamentation.

From this it follows that it is not the product itself that is subject to design protection, but the outwardly visible appearance of the product. Therefore, while the product itself might enjoy patent protection, the shape or appearance of this product can be additionally protected. Application for design protection may be filed for a great diversity of products, including articles of daily use, household goods, furniture, the design of a watch, the housing of a computer or of a technical machine, a camera or a watch or clock. In principle, design protection can even be applied for medical equipment, toys, dolls, and also for items of clothing and decorative articles. The nature of ornamentation itself is eligible for design protection.

Application may be filed for registration of a design for any industrial or handicraft object, including packaging or fittings, graphic symbols or typographical typefaces. Application can also be filed to register parts of a product, such as the handle of a coffee cup even if this handle is not available as a product in its own right. It is often assumed that only "small" things can be the subject matter of design protection. This does not hold true as, in principle, application can be filed to register even the design of an entrance gate, a garden fence or even parts of a building.

In most countries a design is in effect for a maximum of 25 years and constitutes, as do other industrial protection rights, a part of a company's assets. In practice, the value design protection is frequently underestimated. There are many products that do not distinguish themselves technically from other products or which are not patentable, due to the subject matter itself, or its knowledge in the public domain. It is often only the design of such a product that distinguishes it from another product. Design protection in this case, prevents imitation. Furthermore, if one considers that design protection is relatively simple to obtain, it is all the more advisable to comprehensively protect a product, with a patent or utility model, trademark protection and design protection.

5.2.2
National and International Protection of Designs

As with other industrial protection rights, the principle of territoriality applies to design protection, and each protection right is only valid in the country in which it is applied for and registered. Similarly, there are also different routes for the acquisition of design protection, through application to national, Community design and Hague design offices.

In several of these systems, if a design has been made public prior to application, there is a grace period extending 12 months prior to the filing date for design registration. Generally for this grace period to apply the public disclosure must trace back to the applicant or his predecessor in title.

Applications for national designs are filed at the national patent office of a country and are subject to national legal provisions. Whilst in most countries design protection has its own legal regulations, this is part of patent law in the USA, and consequently, the term "design patent" is used in the USA. With a Community Design, protection is obtained in the entire European Union with one unitary protection right. The Community Design regulations differentiate between Unregistered and Registered Community Design. The Community Design is only registered if application has been filed at the Harmonisation Office (OHIM) and the design registered there.

Unregistered Community Design grants informal design protection if the design has been disclosed to the public within the European Union. Disclosure may take the form of business dealings, catalogues, brochures and also presentations at trade fairs, on the Internet or via similar media. If an unrestricted group of persons, particularly professional experts, have had the opportunity to take note of the design, then the designer may plead an Unregistered Community Design. Such design protection does not require any formal registration at an office, but merely proof of this public disclosure. The term of protection of such an Unregistered Community Design commences on the date on which it was made available to the public within the European Union and runs for 3 years. It is possible to file application formally at the OHIM and to have the design subsequently registered as a Registered Community Design. The maximum term of protection granted is then 25 years.

The Hague Design refers to the international lodgement of industrial designs and models with WIPO. Unlike IR trademarks, the applicant of a Hague design can apply directly to WIPO without reference to a national registration, and so may protect a design in several countries with a single application and fee. The Hague system also simplifies the management of the industrial design, since it is possible to record subsequent changes and to renew registration through a simple single procedural step. The basis for the international lodgement of designs or models at the WIPO is the Hague Convention established in 1925, which currently has 40 member signatories. The enforcement of protection against third parties is in accordance with the national law of each of these countries.

5.2.3
How and Where are Designs Registered?

The classification of designs is formally laid out in the "Locarno Agreement Establishing an International Classification for Industrial Designs", which was concluded in 1968 in order to divide all designs clearly into categories. Aside from unregistered Community Designs, a design is entered in the relevant design register at the patent and trademark office of each country or at an international office (e.g. OHIM or WIPO) by means of filing application for registration of the design.

For registration purposes, a design must be new which means that it must not be the same as any design which has already been made available to the public. It must have individual character such that the overall impression it produces on an informed user of the design, differs from the overall impression produced on such a user by any design which has already been made available to the public. It is not possible to register a design which is concerned only with how a product works, or for parts of complex products that are not visible in normal use, or which is contrary to national law or morality.

Any natural person or legal entity is entitled to file application for a design, and the designer need not be applicant. However, the designer has the right to be mentioned in the application for a Community Design. Stating the name of the designer is also obligatory in some countries.

The application for registration of a design must also contain a designation for the design and a reproduction of the design itself. This reproduction is extremely important since it is this lodged reproduction that is decisive in determining the scope of protection of the design. If the reproduction of the design is poor or does not reflect all of its aesthetically distinctive features, the ability to successfully enforce protective rights can be hindered. As a result, virtually all patent offices accept several reproductions of the same design from different perspectives, so that the design is recognisable in great detail. Moreover, the design must be classified according to the Locarno classification system. However, it is not necessary to describe the object in full detail and the only requirement is that the product must be assigned to one of the classes. The purpose of the classification is not for calculating fees, but rather for administration, classification and to facilitate searching of individual designs.

In the case of national applications and the Community Design, fees are calculated by the number of designs for which protection is sought. The number of reproductions of each design does not generally play a role. Application for a Hague Design is filed at the WIPO. The application must include the name of the applicant, a description of the design, together with a reproduction of the design itself in various presentation formats, and a list of countries for which protection is sought. The costs of an international lodgement according to the Hague Design Convention are based upon the number of designs, the presentation format, in colour or black/white, and the respective countries, and may be calculated online at the WIPO website.

Many countries also provide for multiple applications, by which it is possible to protect several designs in one application. When applying for a Community Design, an unlimited number of designs can be lodged as long as they belong to the same Locarno class. Should the products fall into different Locarno classes, the applicant would be asked by the OHIM to separate the multiple applications, resulting in additional fees. Multiple applications are of considerable importance since different designs of a single product can be protected within the scope of one single application. Therefore, a manufacturer of lamps is able to obtain protection for 10 lampshades of different designs in just one application, greatly reducing the application fees. After registration of such a design, design rights come into existence that are legally independent of each other, and which can be asserted, transferred, licensed or ruled-upon individually. Upon expiry of the term of protection, the protection of each individual design must be renewed.

5.2.4
Implementation of Design Rights

In principle, the owner of a registered or unregistered design is entitled to assert claims against an infringer for forbearance and compensation for damages. However, it should be noted that when enforcing design rights, at least in Europe but also in many other countries, the fundamental elements of protection are not examined by the patent offices. Instead, in the event of a dispute, the material conditions of protection, novelty and originality, are examined before a civil court. If a design does not meet these criteria, the dispute may be lost, and the design removed from the register.

6
Licensing

Jan Dirk Heerma

Patent and other intellectual property rights (collectively: "IP rights") confer exclusivity to their owners and allow them to gain financial profit by selling a unique product. The investment required to make a profit through the development of a marketable product however, can be high, and may require skills and assets that are not accessible to the independent inventor, or even to small companies. Indeed large companies have invested heavily to achieve such development, manufacturing and marketing capabilities. This chapter considers the structure of an IP licence; a mechanism which permits the owner of IP rights to leverage these resources, and to avoid the full costs of further development of the invention.

The inventor could sell the IP rights outright for an agreed sum of money. Indeed, such a sale would be a simple legal process. It is difficult, however, to agree a purchase price when neither party has a complete picture of the market potential for products incorporating the invention. Will the invention become a best seller, or indeed will it ever be commercialised at all? The purchaser will hesitate to pay too much for IP rights that cannot be commercially used while the seller will be reluctant to sell the IP rights at a price that is based merely on the probability of success. A licence is a flexible instrument that captures the needs and fears of both the inventor and licensee.

Licence agreements are also a flexible instrument in dense technology areas, in which overlapping patents prevent products coming to market; it may well be that one party cannot use its IP rights without infringing those of another. In such a case, cross-licence agreements, whereby each party grants a licence to its IP rights to the other party, are employed to liberate the market. Such cross licences have become increasingly important, and many technology areas are dense with a network of overlapping patents. Such cross-licences help to settle and avoid expensive litigation.

The following overview concentrates on simple licence agreements. It should be noted, however, that a licence is often one of several elements of other agreements establishing a co-operation, such as research agreements, development agreements, joint-venture agreements and the like. The issues addressed below have to be addressed in all these agreements.

Intellectual Property Management. Claas Junghans, Adam Levy
Copyright © 2006 WILEY-VCH Verlag GmbH & Co. KGaA, Weinheim

6.1
Licence Agreements – an Overview

6.1.1
Introduction to Licensing

The basic structure of a licence agreement is simple: the owner of IP rights (the "licensor") allows the other party (the "licensee") to use its IP rights. The formal IP rights remain with the licensor, but the licensee may utilise them to a specified extent. The licensee's rights are often restricted to certain territories, to specific utilisations or to specific fields of use. For example, a licence may be restricted to sale and production of handheld devices in Japan only. In this case, if the licensee sells products based on the IP rights in any country other than Japan or produces or sells any products other than handheld devices, the licensor's IP rights are infringed. In exchange for the permission to use the rights, the licensee commits to pay a consideration to the licensor. Usually, at least a major part of such consideration is linked to the licensee's sales of products generated by using the IP rights. The licensor's share of such revenues is called "royalty". Such flexible consideration reduces the risk for the licensee, compared to an outright payment. On the other hand, it allows the licensor to share the economic benefit if products based on the IP rights become a best seller. In many cases, the royalty is combined with fixed payments to be made by the licensee irrespective of sales.

Drafting and negotiating licence agreements, particularly trans-national licence agreements, is very complex, and a specialised lawyer should always be consulted. The following overview, therefore, is intended to introduce the core issues within a licence agreement and to prepare the reader for discussions with business partners and lawyers.

6.1.2
Subject

All IP rights can be subject to a licence: patents and utility models, trademarks, design rights, copyrights (including software), and even personality rights. Licences can also be granted with regards to future IP rights, provided that these rights are clearly defined. In fact, most research and development agreements provide for either transfers or license of future IP rights generated in the collaboration.

Furthermore, although it is not a right, know-how may be the subject of a licence. From a legal perspective, the owner of know-how is generally not able to exclude all others from its use, subject to contractual or statutory duties of confidentiality and non-use. From a practical point of view, however, the owner of know-how may exclude all others by keeping this knowledge secret. As long as know-how remains secret, it has an economic value. In order to facilitate development of the invention, and to maximise the value of IP, most patent licence agreements also extend to additional know-how related to the patents.

A pending patent application does not grant any exclusivity rights, but may nevertheless be included within a licence agreement. The applicant may not prohibit anyone from making commercial use of the underlying invention until a patent is granted. However, in most jurisdictions, upon disclosure of the invention in the course of the filing process of the patent, the applicant may claim a statutory compensation from anyone making commercial use of the invention. Such compensation has to be repaid in case the application is rejected or withdrawn or later invalidated. Therefore, when negotiating a licence in a pending application, the parties should be very precise in what they want: Do they only want to agree which compensation is "reasonable"? Or do they want to grant a licence in the future patent, if any? Or does the licensee want to acquire a licence regardless of whether a patent is granted or not? It may be sensible to agree on an adjustment of fees in case no patent is granted.

The following overview concentrates on the core issues of licences on patents and technical know-how. Licence agreements on future patents and utility models have the same structure. Licence agreements on copyrights, especially software, trademarks or personality rights are quite different and are beyond the realm of this book.

6.1.3
Scope

The scope of rights granted in a patent licence goes a long way to defining the commercial and geographical application of the invention, and the licensor needs to give careful consideration to the financial and strategic definition of the scope that maximises profit.

At its broadest definition, the licensor may grant a worldwide licence for all utilisations in all fields of use. In many cases the licensor restricts the defined scope in order to retain some rights, or because the licensee does not have the resources to best develop, manufacture and market products using the IP rights in a comprehensive way. Such restriction enables the licensor to grant further licences for other countries or other fields of application.

Territory
As has been observed, patents are always territorial and relate to specific countries only. The extent and scope of protection will depend upon the patent granted in each territory. From the perspective of the licensee, a licence only makes sense in territories where IP rights exist, and a licensee will only pay for the permission of acts that would otherwise constitute an infringement of the licensor's IP rights. Thus, the licensee will seek to limit the territories where royalties fall due. The licensor, on the other hand, may want to limit the territory for which the licence is granted. Territories should be determined as precisely as possible, and for the avoidance of doubt, it may be useful to use a map as attachment to the licence agreement.

Licence agreements often contain a stipulation to the effect that the licence is granted "worldwide". This usually means that the licensee may use the IP rights anywhere in the world; closer review of the agreement will usually reveal that royalties only fall due in such countries where valid IP rights exist. Any provision to the contrary is likely to conflict with applicable competition laws. The only exception to this rule is the licensing of know-how.

As a general rule, the parties may restrict the territory at will. The licensor may, for example, grant a licence to a French company for sale of products in France only and grant a separate licence to a Portuguese company for sale of products in Portugal. However, the licensor should keep in mind that in most countries, IP rights are "exhausted" once a product has been sold. Sale of a product covered by IP rights is a utilisation that requires the IP owner's consent, but only once. This legal principle of exhaustion is applicable in most jurisdictions. The idea of this principle is that a product is only marketable if the purchaser may resell it. Exhaustion usually does not transcend national borders and reselling a product in another country will require the IP owner's consent. However, in this regard the European Union is to be seen as one country. Once a product has been sold legally within a European Union country, it can be freely sold within the entire zone. The owner of the IP rights in question does not have any legal means to prohibit such resale. IP rights are "exhausted" once a product has been sold within the European Union. Therefore, in this example, the licensor cannot prevent the Portuguese licensee's customers from selling the products in France. In practical terms, this makes it impossible to grant an exclusive licence once another licence has been granted in the European Union, even if the licences refer to different areas, and licensors tend to treat the European Union as a single territory.

Utilisations

A patent, subject to the applicable jurisdiction in question, usually confers a variety of rights to its owner. In the case in which a product is the subject of the patent, the owner may prevent all third parties from making, offering, putting on the market or using such product, or importing or stocking the product for these purposes. If a procedure is the subject of the patent, the owner may prevent all third parties from using such process, from offering the process for use and from making, offering, putting on the market or using products obtained by such process. These acts that would constitute a patent infringement are usually referred to as "utilisations".

In a licence agreement, the licensor may restrict the licensee's rights as to the utilisations of the IP rights. For example, he may restrict the licensee's right to production only, to further development only, or to sale, marketing and distribution only. If, for example, the licensor only needs a manufacturer and is going to market the product himself (contract manufacturing), he will not grant a licence for any other use than manufacturing. If the licence agreement does not contain such restriction, the licence is likely to be deemed to be granted for all such utilisations.

Field of Use

In many cases, IP rights may be used in different fields of use. Different to the term "utilisation", "field of use" is not a legal term but a commercial term and refers to different applications in different markets. For example, an active ingredient of a drug may be used for the therapy of cancer as well as the therapy of rheumatism. In such a case, the licensor may want to grant different licences for different indications and restrict each licence to a certain field of use. Again, if the licence agreement does not contain such restriction, the licence is likely to be deemed to be granted for all such fields of use. Such fields of use should be carefully defined.

6.1.4
Exclusivity

From a commercial point of view, there are two different forms of licences: the exclusive licence and the non-exclusive licence. If the licensee is the only one allowed to use the IP rights in the defined scope, the licence is an "exclusive licence". Since the exclusivity always refers to the scope of the licence, the owner of IP rights may well grant several exclusive licences. He may, for example, grant an exclusive licence to licensee A for the US, an exclusive licence to licensee B for the EU and an exclusive licence to licensee C for the rest of the world. If the licensor reserves his rights to grant the same rights to another licensee, the licence is "non-exclusive". An exclusive licence is more valuable for the licensee, because the licensee does not face competitors using the same IP rights. The consideration for an exclusive licence will therefore be much higher than for a non-exclusive one.

The term "exclusive licence" generally implies that the licensor himself may not use the IP rights, while the term "sole licence " is used to describe a licence where the licensor retains the right to use the IP rights. Such terminology is not always used in the same way, and may be subject to different interpretations, and it should always be clearly determined if, and to what extent, the licensor retains any rights to use the IP rights.

6.1.5
Term and Termination

Effective Date

As a general rule, unless otherwise agreed, a licence agreement becomes effective upon exchange of signatures of all parties. In some countries, usually developing countries, a licence agreement will only become effective upon approval of the competent public authorities. The parties should carefully check whether such approval is required.

The parties may agree on other effective dates, or may agree on conditions, such as financing, that must be met before the agreement takes effect. In this case the licensor must ensure that no know-how is exchanged before the licence agreement becomes effective.

Ordinary Term

A licence agreement either has a fixed term or an unlimited term. In the absence of any other agreement, a fixed term licence runs until the end of the period and is then automatically terminated without notice. Unless otherwise stated, it can only be terminated under extraordinary circumstances. Unlimited term agreements can be terminated by either party. Most countries have little or no statutory or case law as regards the termination period for licence agreements. The details of termination for unlimited term agreements should therefore be carefully agreed. In many cases it may be sensible to define a minimum term.

Licence agreements usually run for a long term. The licensee has to invest either in developing the invention or in manufacturing, and in order to justify this investment a long-term agreement is required. The licensee of a patent is willing to pay royalties only to the extent that patent protection exists. Therefore, the term of patent licence agreements is usually linked with the expiry of the patents. The licence agreement terminates when the last of the licensed patents expires in the last country, usually 15 to 20 years after filing. Know-how agreements usually terminate or can be terminated upon the know-how becoming publicly known.

What happens, however, if an application for a patent is licensed and no patent is granted or if a patent is licensed and is later declared void? In this case, it turns out that the licensor did not, in fact, grant any rights. On the other hand, the licensee had a factual position that allowed the use of an invention in a situation where competitors did not have such an opportunity. Therefore, as a general rule, a licence agreement will expire upon a final and binding decision on the invalidity of the patent. No new royalties will accrue, but royalties accrued or paid will not be reimbursed. This principle may not apply in all jurisdictions and should be detailed in the licence agreement.

Termination for Material Breach or Default

Most agreements provide for a right for each party to terminate the agreement extraordinarily if the other party is in material breach of the agreement. It is sensible to set out in detail what is to be considered a material breach. Termination of a licence agreement is a very harsh consequence for the licensee in light of the investments he made, and the licensee should seek to agree a grace period, so that each party can only terminate the agreement if the other party fails to remedy the breach within a certain time after receipt of written notice.

When an exclusive licence is granted, the licensor should seek protection from licensee underperformance. To a large extent, the licensor's revenue from the licence agreement depends on the licensee's sales. If the licensee undertakes few efforts in that regard, the licensor will receive little royalties but is restricted by exclusivity from granting further licences. In such a case, it is helpful if the parties have agreed on sales targets and the licensor can either terminate the entire agreement or revert to a non-exclusive licence in case the sale targets are not met. The licensee, on the other hand, will strongly resist such provisions arguing that a failure to achieve sales targets is not necessarily the licensee's fault. There is much room for negotiations in this regard, and no standard solution exists.

Termination for Insolvency

In case of insolvency of the licensee, the licensor will often want to terminate the licence agreement because of the fear that, due to insolvency proceedings, royalty payments to the licensor will decrease. Therefore licence agreements usually contain a provision either to the effect that each party may terminate the agreement in case of insolvency of the other party or to the effect that the agreement is terminated upon this event without further notice. The later provision is rarely sensible. Each party should seek to retain its decision whether it wants to terminate the agreement upon the other party becoming insolvent, or whether it wants to proceed with the insolvency receiver. For the licensee, it often does not even make a difference whether the licensor is insolvent or not.

From a legal point of view, the validity of such provisions providing for extraordinary termination rights or automatic termination is often doubtful, depending on the applicable insolvency law in the country in which the insolvent party resides. The best the licensor can do is to negotiate a termination right in the case that the licensee, whether solvent or not, does not meet agreed sales targets.

One other problem is often neglected: in case one party becomes insolvent, applicable insolvency law often provides that the insolvency receiver may terminate the licence agreement, whatever the agreement says. This may put the other party in a very unfortunate position, having already made material up-front or milestone payments. In such a case, the insolvency receiver is likely to terminate the agreement and renegotiate the royalties. Therefore, the effects of insolvency should be carefully investigated when entering into the licence agreement. If appropriate, the licensee may seek for a security *in rem* for its rights, for example by means of a pledge of IP rights. Such security is subject to the laws of the jurisdiction governing the IP rights in question, so one usually has to face a variety of different concepts. However, in many jurisdictions a bilateral agreement stating that the IP rights are pledged as security for a certain claim is possible.

6.1.6
Consideration

In exchange for granted IP rights the licensor expects compensation. Such compensation can take the form of payments or any other claim such as a cross-licence of certain rights of the licensee, shares, or options. Some jurisdictions, notably countries with an Anglo-Saxon law tradition, require that a consideration is made, but in the main, a licence without any consideration is valid. The nature and amount of such compensation depends much on the individual needs of the parties. Some of the most common instruments are set out below. They can be combined at will and such combinations are very common. The most common consideration is a royalty, i.e. a payment that falls due upon sale of products gen-

erated by using the licensed IP rights. Such payments usually fall due at a relatively late stage, and often the licensor will require cash at an earlier stage. In such a
case, the parties may agree on up-front payments, i.e. payments that are due upon
execution of the licence agreement, or on milestone payments, i.e. payments that
are due once certain steps in development or marketing have been reached.

Royalties

Royalties are the easiest way to link payments made to the licensor to the financial
gain from the IP rights made by the licensee. They are based on the products sold
covered by the licensed IP rights and/or embodying the technology. A royalty can
either refer to the number of products sold by the licensee (for example € 1.40 per
product sold) or to the licensee's revenues with the product (for example 4 % of
the net sales of the product). A royalty referring to the volume of products sold is
relatively easy to control, and it makes the licensor independent of prices and currency fluctuation. On the other hand, a royalty referring to revenues is a more
flexible instrument because it gives the licensee freedom to adapt its sales prices
to market conditions and protects the licensor from inflation.

Sometimes parties base royalties not on revenues but on profits. The idea is
that a royalty based on profit reflects even better the economic benefits conferred
to the licensee. Any licensor should strongly resist such a structure, however. The
revenue of a product is a figure that can be determined relatively easily, whereas
profit is a more nebulous concept; costs have to be allocated, and it is very hard to
differentiate between costs directly allocated to the revenues and general over-
head. Even if the parties should succeed in agreeing principles as how to allocate
general costs, this figure still can easily be manipulated.

Royalty percentage rates are hugely influential in determining the value of a
licence agreement. Rates depend largely on the industry in question. They usually
range from 0.1% to 10% and may, in exceptional cases, be lower or exceed these
percentages. In many cases, the parties will not agree on a fixed percentage but
on a percentage schedule, differentiating between products and markets, and a
'stepped' royalty rate, in which the rate is dependent upon net sales. In a combined patent and know-how licence agreement it is sensible to differentiate between countries where patent protection exists and countries where no such protection exists, and only know-how is protected. In addition, the parties may agree
that IP rights notwithstanding, the presence of direct competition in a market
impacts on royalty rates. Thus, royalty clauses in major licence agreements often
become extremely complex and may easily extend over several pages. In such a
case, it is sensible to agree on a sample calculation and attach it to the agreement.
In Box 8, an elaborated clause from a combined patent and know-how licence
agreement in the biotech sector is shown, which differentiates between countries
where patent protection exists and other countries where only know-how is protected.

Box 8

Section 5.03 As further consideration for the acquisition by Licensee of the rights to Licensed Patent under this Agreement Licensee shall pay Licensor the following royalties on total worldwide annual Net Sales in those countries of the Territory in which there is a granted Licensed Patent not held to be invalid or otherwise unenforceable by a court or other legal administrative tribunal from which no appeal is or can be taken, which covers Products at the time such Net Sales occur and where Licensee has exclusive commercialization rights in relation to same:

Annual Net Sales less than and up to and including $300m	10%
Annual Net Sales above $300m and up to and including $500m	12%
Annual Net Sales above $500m and up to and including $800m	13%
Annual Net Sales above $800m	15%

Section 5.04 As further consideration for the acquisition by Licensee of the rights to Licensed Know-How under this Agreement:

(a) Licensee shall pay Licensor the following royalties on total worldwide annual Net Sales in those countries of the Territory which are not subject to the royalty obligation outlined in Section 5.03, and where Licensee has exclusive commercialization rights in respect of Product:

Annual Net Sales less than and up to and including $300m	10%
Annual Net Sales above $300m and up to and including $500m	12%
Annual Net Sales above $500m and up to and including $800m	13%
Annual Net Sales above $800m	15%

(b) Licensee shall pay Licensor the following royalties on total worldwide annual Net Sales in those countries of the Territory where Licensee does not have exclusive commercialization rights in respect of Product as a result of any generic competition in such country or countries:

Annual Net Sales less than and up to and including $300m	4.5%
Annual Net Sales above $300m and up to and including $500m	5.5%
Annual Net Sales above $500m and up to and including $800m	6%
Annual Net Sales above $800m	7%

Section 5.05 For the avoidance of doubt, an example drawn up by the Parties of how Section 5.03 and 5.04 might be applied in practice is attached as Appendix G.

When royalty is linked to revenues, the parties must agree on a definition of "Net Sales". Net Sales exclude VAT, but a number of other questions need to be addressed: Does the term refer to payments received or invoiced? How about costs of packaging, customs, freight, insurance, amounts repaid or credited by reason of rejections and defects, retroactive price reductions or compulsory payments and rebates? A sophisticated licensee will seek to deduct such payments from the revenues and a sophisticated licensor will seek to agree on a cap of such costs. Often the licensed IP rights are required for one component of the final product sold only. In such a case, it has to be determined whether only the price of the component is the basis for the determination of the Net Sales or the entire final product. Intra-group sales must also be carefully treated. In the absence of other agreement, the royalty falls due upon first sale of the product by the licensee, whether sold to an independent party or to a company belonging to the licensee. Such intra-group sales prices are often far below market prices, and a sophisticated licensor will seek to include a provision that intra-group sales shall not be taken into account for determining the net sales but that the final sale by the licensee's affiliate to an independent third party shall be the basis for computing the net sales.

Minimum royalties that fall due irrespective of the licensee's sales protect the licensor from licensee underperformance. This is of vital importance in the case of an exclusive licence because the licensor is prevented from granting further licences within the scope. If no minimum royalties are agreed, it is important that the licensor can terminate the agreement if sales targets are not met. Otherwise, it is possible that the licensor will receive no payment for valuable IP rights.

Parties must agree a due date for the royalties. In practical terms royalties are either due once a year or quarterly. The parties should agree on the currency that is used for determining the net sales and the currency that is used for payments. Such currencies do not necessarily have to be the same. The effect of a choice of currency should be carefully assessed in both cases, to protect against currency fluctuations.

The licensee must be obliged to render account on its sales of the products in question to the licensor and the licensor must have the right to request an audit of such calculation. Such clauses are standard, and the only cause for negotiation is which party bears the cost of an audit. Usually, the licensee will be obliged to bear the costs if the audit reveals a deviation from the figures presented by the licensee of more than 1 to 5 %.

6.2
Sub-Licences

If the licensee is entitled to grant sub-licences, as is often the case with exclusive licences, then the question arises how to determine the licensor's share in such profits. Two principles of measurement are common: Either the parties agree that the agreed royalty also falls due in case a product is sold by the sub-licensee. In this case, the licensee is well advised to request a royalty that matches or exceeds the royalty paid by him to the original licensor. This method usually applies if the licence and the sub-licence are granted for the same product.

The alternative method is to agree on a share in the licencee's revenues from such out-licensing, whether royalties, up-front payments, milestone payments or any other payments. Naturally, the distribution of such revenues will be different to that agreed in the initial royalty agreement, because few costs will have to be taken into account. While profit margins from product sales may be of the order of 10%, those from royalties or other sub-licensee fees may be closer to 100%. Such calculation is sensible if the parties are not sure of the cost structure of the final product, as will often be the case for additional or new fields of application.

Both methods can be combined to the effect that the licensor's share in revenues is capped at the amount the licensor would have received from royalties if the licensee had sold the products himself.

6.3
Up-Front Payments

Up-front payments, which are lump sum fees paid upon execution of the licence agreement, may either replace or augment royalties. The attractive aspect of up-front payments is their simplicity: the licensor does not have to control the licensee's sales, nor to worry about the licensee's future liquidity or the success of the sales efforts of the licensee. On the other hand, up-front payments tend to be smaller than the amounts paid as royalties. Up-front payments therefore usually only replace royalties in deals with a low volume or in deals in which the licence is only part of an overall package. Since such payments are intended to represent the value for the licence during the entire term, it should be determined whether they are refundable in case of an early termination. If material amounts are to be paid, such deal is risky for the licensee: if the licensor becomes insolvent, the licence may be terminated and the up-front payment may be lost.

If up-front payments are made in addition to royalties, they may be a consideration for know-how disclosed ("disclosure fee") or a reimbursement of costs incurred ("signing fee"). In many cases up-front payments have a financing function and are based on the liquidity requirements of the licensor. Future royalties based on the sale of as-yet undeveloped products do not generate immediate cash-flow for the licensor. If, for example, a small biotech company out-licenses a drug that still is in research, it may take years before the first products are sold. The biotech company will require interim sources of finance. In making up-front payments, some of the product development risk is assumed by the licensee, and the licensee will only be willing to make such up-front payments in exchange for a reduction in the ultimate royalty rate. Again, the parties should determine under which circumstances the payments are refundable and the licensee should take into account the effects of a possible insolvency of the licensor. It should be determined to what extent, if any, the payments may be off-set against future royalties.

6.4
Milestone Payments

Milestone payments are common structures to allow the licensee to progressively fund the development of the IP rights and to reward the licensor for technical development. If, for example, the further development of a drug until marketing approval by the competent authorities will cost about 50 million €, the licensee will not pay 50 million € at once, but start with 10 million €, pay another 15 million € upon the successful first tests in the clinics, and so forth. Much is open for negotiation in this regard. The parties should ensure the milestone events, which trigger payments, are defined as precisely as possible.

6.5
Non-Cash Consideration

In addition to, or in replacement of, payments, the licensee may be obliged to a non-cash consideration. The most common case is that the licensee in turn grants a "cross-licence" in its own IP rights to the licensor or in improvements or new applications of the licensed IP rights. Such agreements have an anti-competitive element and therefore need careful review under applicable competition law (see Section 6.10 for details).

Sometimes a licensor acquires shares in the licensee with a view to entering into a strategic alliance or vice versa. Such a structure will usually require a separate agreement with the shareholders of the respective party since they are the only ones who can validly transfer shares.

6.6
Taxation of Consideration

As a general rule, the licensor has to pay income taxes for royalties and other fees received in the country in which it is resident. In addition, the licensor may be taxable in the country where the licensee is resident. In fact, many countries oblige the licensee to withhold a percentage of the fees payable to a foreign licensor. Such withholding tax usually ranges between 5 to 20 % of the payments to be made. However, most double taxation treaties provide that licence fees are taxable only in the recipient's country and that no withholding tax applies. Within the European Union, a European Directive obliges all member states to refrain from applying any withholding tax to licence fees, but this directive has not been executed by all member states (for example not in Germany) and, therefore, the tax situation is doubtful even between certain member states of the European Union. Licensors often try to shift this problem to the licensee by a clause that provides that all payments are to be made net of any withholding taxes. This clause may be invalid under the laws of the state in which the licensee is resident, and the taxation of all payments made under trans-national licence agreements should be carefully assessed by the licensor.

6.7
Representations and Warranties

Licensing deals contain an inherent element of risk. Even if the claimed IP rights are registered in the name of the licensor, the licensee cannot be sure whether the licensor really owns such rights, and even if the original inventors are identified, one cannot be sure that there are not additional inventors. The licensor cannot be sure that the IP rights remain valid. All of this is in addition to inherent techno-logical uncertainty as to whether future products will be developed. The licensor, on the other hand, is also not sure about these issues and will be reluctant to give these representations and warranties. Still, there are a number of issues where the licensee should seek a warranty. One has to distinguish between hard warran-ties where the guarantor warrants for a fact or non-existence of a fact regardless of its own fault or negligence and soft warranties where the warranty is restricted to the guarantor's best knowledge. It has to be negotiated for each individual war-ranty whether it is "hard" or "soft". The content of the most important and most common warranties is set out below.

6.7.1
Ownership

The core issue is that the licensor owns the IP rights in question. If IP rights have not been validly acquired from an employer or from any other owner, they cannot be out-licensed. This may become a major issue when IP rights have been trans-ferred several times. If a transfer in the chain of rights is invalid or does not cover all of the rights in question, the licensor is not the owner of the IP rights. It is wise for the licensee to investigate this and to perform a "due diligence" and review all previous ownership documents. Since the licensee cannot be sure that the documents provided to him are conclusive, such due diligence does not replace a warranty. Thus, a hard warranty to the effect that the licensor owns full title in the licensed IP rights is very common.

6.7.2
Third Parties' Rights

A licensor will also seek for a warranty to the effect that the IP rights can be used without infringement of third parties' rights. However, this can, to a certain extent, be investigated by means of a patent due diligence, and the licensor does not necessarily have superior knowledge. Therefore, there is usually some arguing about representations and warranties of this kind. Since even the most thorough research cannot exclude that an IP right is invalidated due to third party rights that have not yet been revealed or published, it is uncommon to have hard warranties as regards third parties' rights in licence agreements, and the licensee should seek protection by other means. The most common instrument is a clause to the effect that the royalties to be paid are decreased in the case that royalties must be paid to another party for the same product. In case IP rights are invalidated, the question is whether the technology is still protected by secret know-how. If not, no further royalties should be due. If know-how is still in place, the royalties may be decreased. All this should be agreed in advance.

6.7.3
Other

There is much room for negotiation as regards other representations or warranties such as merchantability, technical fitness or fitness for particular purpose. Whether or not the licensor is willing to give such warranties very much depends on the stage of development of the IP rights in question. When the products still have to be developed, the licensor will not be willing to give such warranty, while a party in-licensing a marketable product will consider such warranty to be essential.

6.8
Maintenance and Prosecution of IP Rights

Ownership of out-licensed IP rights remains with the licensor. Therefore, in the absence of any provision to the contrary in the licence agreement, the licensor must maintain such rights and pay all fees as they fall due, and must defend them against challenges from third parties. The licensor therefore runs the risk that the fees to be paid for maintenance of the IP right and the cost of litigation exceed the royalties to be paid for such IP rights, and should either seek reimbursement of this cost from the licensee or have the right to either abandon or transfer IP rights.

It is doubtful whether a licensor must prosecute infringements from third parties, and in some jurisdictions an exclusive licensee may, by law, prosecute infringements from third parties. The parties should avoid uncertainty and determine a clear responsibility in this regard. It is of vital importance to the exclusive licensee that any infringements from third parties are prosecuted, as they are likely to interfere with the licensee's position in the market. IP litigation is likely to take place in several countries at a time and is very costly. On the other hand, revenues from such litigation may also be remarkable. In this scenario, the parties usually agree that one party has the final responsibility for prosecuting the IP rights but both parties share costs and revenues from such litigation. In case one party does not want to bear its portion of the costs, the other party has the right to take over both its share in costs and revenues from litigation.

6.9
Confidentiality

In a pure know-how licence agreement it is essential that the licensee undertakes not to make disclosures to third parties and ceases to use know-how once the licence agreement is terminated. In fact, most licence agreements have an element of know-how involved, and, therefore contain confidentiality provisions. Such clauses not only restrict either or both parties' rights to disclose confidential information to third parties, they also restrict the use of confidential information for their own purposes. The parties must determine which information they deem confidential; for example, only information which is clearly marked as confidential or any information that is confidential by its nature. Usually, the disclosing party wants to restrict access to the confidential information to persons with a need to know and the agreement should clearly state this.

There are a number of standard carve-outs in confidentiality clauses: If the confidential information is no longer confidential, if it is received from a third party not bound by a duty of confidentiality, or if it was already known prior to disclosure, the recipient of such information will not be bound by his duties for confidentiality and non-use. The only carve-out that is usually the subject of negotiations is a provision to the effect that the confidentiality restrictions do not apply to information which is independently developed. While such a limitation is reasonable from the recipient's perspective, the disclosing party faces a problem of evidence. How is the disclosing party able to control what was independently developed? The disclosing party should carefully assess whether it can agree to such provision.

Determining the damage if there has been a breach of confidentiality or non-use obligations is very difficult. Therefore, the disclosing party may want to agree on a contractual penalty. In some jurisdictions, contractual penalties are unenforceable but similar instruments such as liquidated damages are common. In any case, contractual penalties or liquidated damages are unusual and the party requiring such a clause should be prepared for lengthy discussions.

When negotiating a licence agreement, it is likely that some know-how is disclosed prior to entering into the final agreement. Therefore, it is common to execute a separate confidentiality agreement at an early stage of negotiations. Once a licence agreement is concluded, the secrecy agreement is usually replaced by a corresponding secrecy clause within the licence agreement.

6.10
Competition Law

6.10.1
General Principles

Most industrialised countries have laws which prohibit agreements that have an adverse effect on competition. Under these competition laws, agreements may be void, or the parties may be subject to material fines. IP rights are, by their nature, anti-competitive because they create a legal monopoly on a certain technology. A licence agreement which effectively grants part of this legal monopoly to the licensee does not generally constitute an infringement of competition law. Often however, licence agreements contain stipulations which have farther reaching effects on competition. For example a licensor could well want to draft an agreement restricting the ability of a licensee to determine the price or volume of product which can be sold, or to develop further products in the same market. Such an agreement is likely to fall foul of competition law.

6.10.2
European Competition Law

The European Union provides an example of how competition law can impact on the detailed terms of an IP licence. Article 81 of the Treaty establishing the European Community ("EC Treaty") prohibits all agreements which may affect trade between member states and which prevent, restrict or distort competition within the common market. The prohibition applies in particular to agreements which directly or indirectly fix purchase or selling prices or limit or control production, markets, technical development, or investment.

The provisions of Article 81 EC Treaty may, however, be declared inapplicable in certain cases. They are not applicable to agreements that do not have an appreciable effect on competition or intra-Community trade. The European Commission provides guidelines with market share thresholds as to when an agreement has an appreciable effect on competition[1] or on intra-Community trade.[2] The Technology Transfer Block Exemption ("TTBER") additionally exempts certain licence agreements from the prohibition of Article 81 EC Treaty.

On 1 May 2004, the process of applying block exemptions in general, as well as the old TTBER itself was completely renewed.[3] It now is the exclusive responsibility of the parties to make sure that their licence agreement complies with European competition law. Unfortunately, the TTBER is very complex and it has become very difficult to determine whether or not a licence agreement complies with this law. The new TTBER distinguishes between competitors and non-competitors, and applies a number of different tests. The general concept is that a licence agreement is exempt from Article 81 EC Treaty if the parties' market share does not exceed certain thresholds and if the agreement does not contain one of the provisions the TTBER lists as "hardcore restrictions" or "excluded restrictions".

---

1) Commission Notice on agreements of minor importance which do not appreciably restrict competition under Art. 81 (1), OJ 2001 C 368/13 (*de-minimis*).

2) Commission Notice Guidelines on the effect on trade concept contained in Art. 81 and 82 of the Treaty, OJ 2004 C 101/7.

3) No. 772/2004 of 27 April 2004 on the application of Article 81 (3) of the EC Treaty to categories of technology transfer agreements

The national competition laws within the European Union have become or will soon become quite similar to European Union's competition laws. In the meantime, however, these laws still differ, and should be investigated in detail.

Market Thresholds

If the parties of a licence agreement are competitors, the agreement will only be exempt from the application of Art. 81 EC Treaty, if the parties' combined market share does not exceed 20 % of the affected technology and product market. If the parties are not competitors, the agreement will be exempt from the application of Art. 81 EC Treaty, if the market share of each of the parties does not exceed 30% of the affected technology and product market. Notwithstanding these thresholds, an agreement is not exempt if it contains so-called "hardcore restrictions" as set out below.

Even if combined market exceeds the threshold set out above, a licence agreement may still be in accordance with Article 81 EC Treaty. There is no presumption that agreements which fall outside the scope of the block exemption are illegal, provided that they do not contain hardcore restrictions as set out below.

Hardcore Restrictions

Some restrictions are deemed to be so anti-competitive that they exclude the application of the TTBER to all provisions of the agreement as a whole. There is a distinction between competitors and non-competitors, and in addition, the TTBER makes a distinction between reciprocal and non-reciprocal agreements. Reciprocal agreements are cross-licences for competing technologies. The hardcore list is stricter for reciprocal agreements.

For competitors, as a general rule, the following restrictions are considered hardcore restrictions:
- restrictions of a party's ability to determine its prices when selling products to third parties,
- limitations of output except non-reciprocal limitations on the output of contract products,
- allocation of markets or customers (with a long list of exceptions),
- obligations limiting the licensee's ability to exploit its own technology, or limiting either parties ability to carry out research and development.

Field of use and product market restrictions are permitted, but territorial restriction is more complicated, and the core problem for a licence agreement is the allocation of markets. This issue arises in any licence agreement where the licensee is granted exclusivity, but the licensor retains some of its rights with a view to a further out-license to a third party. The TTBER distinguishes between active sales (i.e. active marketing and promotion) and passive sales (i.e. sale upon individual request of an unsolicited customer). Restricting passive sales constitutes a hardcore restriction. Restricting active sales is also deemed a hardcore restriction if the third party licensee is a competitor of the licensor. This may sound harsh, but a licensor should bear in mind that for registered IP rights, sales need not be contractually prohibited, if the sale of such products would constitute an infringement of its IP rights. In other words, if a licence is granted for a certain territory only, in the absence of any further provision in the licence agreement, the licensee may only sell products requiring the IP rights in the defined territory, or in territories in which no IP rights exist.

For non-competitors, as a general rule, the following restrictions are considered hardcore restrictions:
- minimum pricing restrictions,
- restrictions on territories or customers to whom the licensee can passively sell the contractual products (with a long list of exceptions),
- restrictions of active or passive sales to end users by a licensee which is a member of a selective distribution system at the retail level.

Excluded Restrictions
Some other restrictions are also exempt from the TTBER, but will, as a general rule, not infect the whole licence agreement:
- grant-back licences obliging the licensee to grant to the licensor an exclusive licence to improvements or new applications of the licensed technology or to assign the rights therein,
- non-challenge clauses obliging the licensee not to challenge the validity of licensor's IP rights,
- where the parties are not competitors, obligations limiting the licensee's ability to exploit its own technology.

6.10.3
US Competition Law

US competition law differs very much from European competition law in its theoretical approach. However, as a general rule, the results under US competition law are usually very similar to those under European competition law. Agreements that are valid under European competition law are likely to be valid under US competition law.

6.11
Governing Law and Dispute Resolution

Each trans-national licence agreement should contain a choice of the applicable law and a mechanism for dispute resolution. While the parties usually negotiate in detail about the financial aspects, these clauses are often considered boilerplate. Their importance, however, can hardly be overestimated. In the worst case, the licence agreement is unenforceable. The pros and cons of the applicable laws in question and the mechanisms for dispute resolution must be carefully investigated in each individual case.

6.11.1
Governing Law

As a general rule, the parties may choose the laws of the country by which their licence agreement is to be governed. Some additional requirements vary from country to country: In European Union member countries, a choice of law clause must be in writing. In the US, the choice of law must be "reasonable".

The choice of law determines the drafting style of the licence agreement. While agreements governed by the laws of a country with an Anglo-Saxon law tradition (English law, the laws of the US states or the law of any state belonging or having belonged to the Commonwealth of Nations) tend to be extremely detailed, agreements governed by continental law traditionally concentrate on the material issues. This is because courts in continental Europe will, as a general rule, investigate the parties' intention while courts in Anglo-Saxon countries will rely on the actual wording of the agreement. However, the Anglo-Saxon drafting style is becoming more popular, even for agreements governed by continental law.

The choice of law is limited to the agreement and its interpretation only. All other aspects of the applicable law are beyond the disposition of the parties: the protection and prosecution of the IP rights themselves will always be governed by the laws of the specific countries. For example, the validity of a US patent can only be challenged within a US court, regardless of the laws that govern the licence agreement. The parties may not choose the applicable competition law, nor the tax regime nor any other public laws. In these regards, they are subject to the laws of the countries where they are resident. Where they act in foreign countries, they will in addition be subject to the laws of these countries. Each party is subject to the laws on insolvency of its own country, despite the fact that such laws may materially affect the enforceability of the licence agreement. In addition, a country will not enforce foreign law where such law is manifestly contrary to public policy of its own law.

Each party usually wants the laws of its own country to govern the agreement – simply because it is more familiar with such law. If it comes to disputes, it is usually much more complicated if foreign law governs the agreement and foreign lawyers must be assigned. In a trans-national licence agreement, however, the parties have to agree on the laws of one country. The predominating party will usually succeed in choosing the laws of its own country for the agreement. US companies in particular, are very reluctant to agree on any other law than US law. Sometimes the parties consider a compromise by either not choosing a law at all or choosing the laws of a third country. These are not favourable solutions. In the first case, it may be hard to determine which law governs at all, and thus it may be hard to interpret the contract at all. If the parties choose the laws of a third country, this may seem a quite well balanced solution, because it is unfavourable for both parties, but it may be that the choice of law is deemed "unreasonable" and not recognized.

6.11.2
Dispute Resolution

Parties tend to seek dispute resolution under the jurisdiction of their own nation's courts. It is unfavourable to file a claim in a foreign state since the claimant has to deal with foreign lawyers and courts, and the parties are often fearful that the courts will be biased towards the resident party.

The most important question is whether or not a court decision can be executed in the country in which the other party is resident. A country will only recognize and enforce a foreign court decision if a treaty is in place with the country in which the court decision was made. This has to be considered for the individual countries in question. Within the European Community, the Brussels I Directive[4] obliges the European Union member countries to recognize and enforce decisions legally made in other European Union member countries, although court decisions that are manifestly contrary to public policy are not recognized. German courts, for example, do not recognize foreign court decisions for punitive damages.

For practical reasons, one should avoid a situation in which a court has to apply foreign law. While it is technically possible that a German court applies English law, this makes litigation extremely complex and the outcome is almost unpredictable because the court will rely on expert opinion with regard to the interpretation of foreign law.

For these reasons, disputes under cross-border licence agreements are usually settled by arbitration. This means that any dispute will not be settled by the courts of the states but by a chosen tribunal. The parties may choose the persons of the arbitrators and elect persons with industry expertise. In arbitration proceedings, the parties can agree on the language of their choice. Arbitration may be faster and cheaper than court proceedings, but as both costs and the time of litigation vary dramatically from country to country, no general rule can be given in this regard. Several institutions exist throughout the world offering arbitration[5] and which one is chosen should be decided on a case-by-case basis.

Again, the most important question is whether the arbitration award will be recognized and enforced in the country in which the other party is resident. Most countries have agreed to either the Convention of Geneva or the Conventions of New York and do recognize arbitration awards, but this has to be verified in the individual case.

4) Directive No 44/2001 dated 22 December 2000, ABlEG No. L 12 dated 16 January 2001

5) International Chamber of Commerce: http://www.iccwbo.org/home/menu_

international_arbitration.asp
Deutsches Institut für Schiedsgerichtsbarkeit: http://www.dis-arb.de/

6.12
Negotiating Licence Agreements

The first step in negotiating a licence agreement is usually the presentation of the technology to the potential licensee. To this end, it may be wise that the potential licensor prepares a document or slide show outlining the IP rights and their commercial application and the advantages of the technology in comparison to competing technologies. This is straight-forward when out-licensing IP rights such as patents. But out-licensing know-how is more complicated. Whilst protecting the secrecy of know-how, the licensor must convince the licensee that such know-how is valuable. It is obvious that it is almost impossible to comply with both requirements. The first step in such a case is to enter into a confidentiality agreement restricting the use of the know-how of the potential licensor. Under no circumstances, the potential licensor should disclose any know-how without having such confidentiality agreement in place. In addition, the licensor should seek not to disclose know-how prior to the effective date of the licence agreement.

The parties should then negotiate the material topics of the licence agreement; its scope, consideration and term. The results should jointly be laid down in writing. Such joint paper is called "letter of intent", "heads of terms" or "memorandum of understanding". It sets out the material content of the anticipated transaction but, as a general rule, is not intended to oblige either party to enter into a final agreement. For avoidance of doubt, the paper should state that the parties do not intend to be legally bound. Even then, depending on the applicable jurisdiction, it may well be that the parties have certain pre-contractual obligations, such as to inform the other party in case they do not wish to proceed with negotiations.

Only then the parties should start to negotiate on the licence agreement itself, and involve lawyers. Licences are lengthy and complicated agreements. The reasons are twofold. Firstly, in most countries, there is little statutory law on the rights and obligations laid out in licence agreement, so these rights and obligations need to be defined in detail. Secondly, licence agreements usually have a long term, and the term is likely to be longer than the negotiating persons are with their respective companies. Details that may be self-explanatory to the negotiators may be far-fetched for someone interpreting the agreement 15 years later.

The parties should agree which party is to present the first draft of the agreement. In many cases, one party will want to save the legal fees for drafting the agreement and leaves it to the other party to present a first draft. However, the right to present the first draft is a very valuable one. Once a draft is presented, the other party has to argue about each and any issue to be amended and explain why they deem such amendment necessary. In addition, the party presenting the first draft will usually be the party making amendments during the course of ongoing negotiations, which again is a favourable role.

Drafting and negotiating a licence takes teamwork and management and the cooperation of scientists and lawyers. Whether or not the lawyers are involved in the negotiation of the licence agreement should be decided on a case-by-case basis. In smaller deals the parties often decide to negotiate among themselves and to involve lawyers only on an internal basis, producing or reviewing drafted documents. In other cases, the lawyers are an integral part of the negotiation, and of creating licence agreements that meet the needs of both licensee and licensor.

6.13
Business Brief

If a patent or other IP right is not used by its owner, a licence agreement is the most likely and useful mode of generating cash flow. Hence, the licence agreement is a very important link in the IP value chain. Licence agreements vary greatly depending on the needs of the parties, specific customs of the industry, particular properties of the licensed IP rights, and other variables. A number of issues, however, should always be addressed.

Scope: the extent to which a licence is granted. The scope of the licence can be limited with regard to territory, the kind of utilisation (research only vs. manufacture only), or the field of use (diagnostics vs. therapeutics; cars vs. aeroplanes etc.).

Exclusivity: a licence can be granted exclusively, or non-exclusively. Exclusivity always refers to the scope of the licence granted, so that the licensor (the "giver" of the licence) may grant several exclusive licenses referring to a different scope.

The **term** or duration of the licence agreement, and possible ways of terminating the agreement for either party if certain expectations are not met. Special consideration should be paid to clauses regulating the insolvency of either party.

Royalties or other consideration: the amount of money the licensor receives, and the modality and conditions of payment. This clause is unlikely to be entirely absent from a licence agreement, but agreements differ greatly in the detail. Since the issue of remuneration is likely to be the most important issue for at least one of the parties involved, care should be taken to anticipate and settle possible conflicts prior to their arising. Revenue-dependent royalties, upfront payments and milestone payments are the most common method of arranging for payment of the licensor.

Warranties: the licensee (the "taker" of the licence) will seek some reduction of the risk arising from the possibility of IP rights being invalid or challenged, and other risks involved in the transaction.

Maintenance and prosecution: The parties need to agree who is responsible for maintaining and enforcing the IP rights that are the basis of the licence agreement.

Competition law: Some clauses of a licence agreement may be unenforceable due to competition law, or even worse, the whole licence agreement may be unenforceable. This is risky when the parties' market shares exceed certain thresholds or when the licence agreement contains certain clauses which are deemed to have a specific anti-competitive effect.

Governing law and **dispute resolution**: Ancillary regulations that are often neglected but may have an enormous impact on the enforceability of the agreement and, thus, the value eventually generated, in case of conflict.

All the above issues should be addressed diligently in any licence agreement.

7
Starting up and Financing Your Venture

Adam Levy

As has been repeated throughout this book, patents are technical legal documents, the purpose of which is economic gain. The patent application and licensing strategies discussed therefore occur within a commercial framework. This chapter addresses the independent inventor who wishes to realise financial gain from his or her creation through developing, licensing or selling the invention. It considers commercialisation strategy, company formation and funding, and eventual exit of the business.

7.1
Risk, Return and Control

Throughout this chapter several key words are repeated; risk, return, control. This trinity defines much of the vision and strategy of the start-up company, and the inventor must continually trade these values against each other. Yet, the circumstances, preferences and attitudes of each inventor will differ and indeed, evolve over time, so there is no simple way to optimise this trade.

The inventor must question his or her attitude to this risk. What personal investment of time and money is to be made in the invention, and what is expected in return? People differ greatly in their attitude to money and what constitutes "enough" money, and to what extent risks are justified to have more money. Whilst every inventor wants to earn a fair and maximal amount from their creation, it is important to understand the risks that underlie this process, and to define a personal strategy of involvement that fits with this risk. Some inventors will be driven by money; some by a desire to create and control an invention; some will be intensely risk-averse, whilst others will be risk-loving. What is presented here is therefore, at best, a framework to help the entrepreneurial inventor to understand his or her own attitudes, and start to plan the future.

Intellectual Property Management. Claas Junghans, Adam Levy
Copyright © 2006 WILEY-VCH Verlag GmbH & Co. KGaA, Weinheim

7.1.1
What is the Return?

Put simply, the return is the money that the inventor manages to realise from the invention, adjusted for time and taxation. Taxation is covered in more depth in Chapter 8 and the relationship between time and money is discussed in depth later in this chapter. Beyond these elements, two key concepts are useful in defining ones own attitude to return:

The Marginal Utility of Money

When one compares the price of a pair of shoes in two stores a 10 € price difference seems more important than it does when comparing the cost of two cars. The 10 € is the same, so why the difference in attitude? The answer lies in the concept of marginal utility – that is to say that the more one has of something, the less meaningful the next additional unit seems. Marginal utility applies also to money. Although the concept of 'too much money' is an alien one to the struggling and penniless entrepreneur, it is important to explore attitudes to money and risk and to identify the point at which additional risk cannot be justified.

Take the example of the young entrepreneur whose company is at the point of making an exclusive agreement from which he can walk away with 1 million €. It is suggested that the inventor tries to make the deal non-exclusive, so that the invention can also be sold elsewhere. If he tries this, it is possible that the deal will fall through, and equally possible that the tactic will work and that the invention will net 3 million €. Logically taking the gamble is rational after all there is a 50% chance of more than doubling the return (in economic terms the Expected Value, or EV is therefore higher at 1.5m Euros). On the other hand, why should the inventor gamble the financial security of 1 million €. Presented with the same odds in a card game would the inventor gamble the same amount of money? The young entrepreneur wisely decides to sign the exclusive agreement.

The young entrepreneur banks his cool 1 million Euros and again has made a great invention. Faced with the same dilemma, but this time with a 5% chance of making 10 million Euros, the inventor chooses to take the considerable gamble (lowering his EV to 0.5m Euros) – after all, an additional 1 million Euros will not radically change his life, whereas an additional 10 million Euros would indeed.

This relationship between risk and return is a phenomenon that inventors, managers and investors must try to understand, to avoid distortions in decision making. The inventor must understand that investors, particularly professional investors with extensive portfolios, may prefer higher return investments despite the additional risk. Inventors must structure shareholder agreements that act to align the risk profiles of investors with their own interests.

Equity

Equity does not refer here to the ownership stakes in a company, but to the overall concept of fairness. The inventor making an invention, investor putting their money at risk or company buying a patent can expect a certain profit, but exceptional profits above this level ask questions of fairness. Whilst the profit-making party will naturally be delighted, there is a feeling of injustice when entering into an agreement that you feel to be one-sided. And yet why should the exceptional profit made by someone else impact on one's own perception of profit? It is human nature to demand this natural justice, and yet it is irrational behaviour.

This behaviour can distort decision-making. Take the high-technology start-up company securing its first investment round. The investors understand the high-risk nature of the technology and it is agreed that the following years will see the company worth £ 3 million or nothing. The inventor has already decided that he just wants to make £ 1m and would take no additional risk to make more money. The investors want to take 1/2 of the company in exchange for their capital investment of £ 100k. The inventor, unable to find funds elsewhere is furious at the level of return that the investors could be making – 15 times their money in just a few years. He fails to see that if the investors do succeed in making this return, he himself, will have made enough money to be happy. He would be foolish to risk this opportunity by not taking the current investment deal, and yet is prepared to jeopardise it by giving voice to his concepts of fairness.

Fairness is a strong human force and one that is an important outcome in a negotiation. Nevertheless, it is important for inventors and investors alike to understand the psychology behind such notions, and to act, as far as possibly, rationally. A failure to do so can lead to the adoption of risk that would not otherwise have been contemplated.

7.1.2
Understanding Risk

Whilst inventors may have a good grasp of the broad concepts of probability, the risk adopted by an inventor in commercialisation of a patent is generally poorly understood. This personal risk is a function of the chance that the project will fail, and the amount of resources invested by the inventor. This book encourages a rational and measured approach to the adoption of controlled and understood risk. The inventor, as far as possible, must understand risk from an objective perspective, make realistic assessments of the likelihood of success, and commit a calculated and commensurate level of personal resource.

Project Risk

Patents are, by their nature, uncharted territory. There is a certain risk, therefore, that they will fail in any number of technological and commercial ways. Technology risk is a function of the specific scientific field and the extent of novelty, and in many areas, precedents exist to describe this risk. In the pharmaceutical field, for example, it is generally agreed that Phase I drugs have a certain likelihood of success, compared to Phase II and Phase III. These figures can then be adjusted based on the extent to which the drug belongs to a new product class or mimics existing drugs.

Commercial risk describes the possibility that despite overcoming its technical milestones, the invention does not become a success, by virtue of the market environment or competition. The Betamax video format for example, was a technical triumph that did not translate into a commercial success. Commercial risks can be moderated to an extent by the right management skills, but are hard to quantify. Inventors and investors must be aware that risk does not end with the success of an invention or patent.

Resource Commitment

Invention itself is a creative act, which is not necessarily risk-taking, in much the same way that rolling dice is not gambling unless money is placed on the outcome. Unless resources are consumed by invention there is similarly no risk. Intent upon development and commercialisation, it is easy for inventors to invest a great deal of time, money and emotional energy in their invention. Inventors must carefully monitor this tendency and make rational decisions with regards to the level of this investment. These considerations should include the opportunity cost of their actions – what else could they be doing or investing in, and indirect costs, such as the impact on family life or current job. The appropriate level of resources to put at risk must be a rational decision, based on personal perspective and circumstance.

Risk Profile

Individual attitudes to risk are hard to pinpoint. Risk-loving or risk-averse behaviour is a result of a multitude of both financial and psychological functions, and is highly personal. As seen in consideration of return, the independently wealthy investor may have a different risk profile to the poor inventor. The need for financial security of a married inventor with children may be different to that of the unmarried inventor, and yet the need for personal security may be less. The professional investor with a portfolio of investments will have a different risk appetite to the inventor with all of his assets tied into a single invention.

The formal agreements that regulate the way in which investors work with the company must be written so as to align the diverse risk profiles of these constituents with those of the inventor.

7.1.3
Managing Risk

Risk can be sought out in balance with return, and the two are often interlinked. The strong and capable organisation is also, however, able to analyse, understand

and manage its risks. Skilled people with toolboxes of management methods can tame and minimise risk whilst maintaining return. The minimisation of risk within an organisation is complex and depends upon a number of factors:

Objective Transparency

In order to fully understand its risks, companies must make objective appraisals based on an entirely honest and transparent approach. Systems must be established to ensure both objectivity and honesty. In a research environment in which progress is praised, for example, it is all too easy for an organisation to believe so strongly in its research that it fails to see its flaws, or to fully position the work within a broader scientific or commercial context. An honest internal communication of risks is essential.

Experience

Risk is measured and managed by people, and not by models. Experienced managers are essential to address, control and minimise risk. Managers make decisions on behalf of shareholders and must do so with as much clarity of risk and potential return as available.

Apply Common Sense to the Unknown

It is the nature of inventive novelty that parts of the technology and its future remain unclear. Rather than trying to precisely analyse the unknown, risk is better managed by making strong approximations, and establishing systems to review and refine these approximations. It is better to be approximately right, than to be precisely wrong.

Discipline

A consistent and rigorous strategy will beat a constantly changing system. Change introduces new and poorly understood and identified risks, and a carefully defined commitment strategy removes this uncertainty.

7.1.4
Control

Small companies without collateral find it difficult to borrow money to fund product development, and as a result, often end up selling equity, or shares, in the company. Whether development necessitates accessing large sums from the capital markets or small sums from family and friends is often beyond the control of the independent inventor. In either case, however, it is important to understand that the ownership and control of the invention is effectively being traded for these resources. With each successive round of fundraising the inventor's share in the company is diluted. A greater sum of money raised, at greater risk, necessitates that a higher level of equity is sold. Ultimately, a company is owned by its shareholders, who control its fate. The extent to which a dilution in equity is translated into a dilution in control depends upon a number of factors.

Retaining Control

An inventor or company founder can retain significant control over the company and the invention in a number of ways.

- Minimise funding requirements.

  By minimising fundraising, founders can retain their share in the company. Given the invention and its technical and commercial environment, however, this retention of control, may prematurely curtail the development of a product and of profit. The founders may be left with control over a failure, rather than a smaller interest in a success.

- Choose compliant investors.

  Initial investors may be predominately friends and family. These non-professional investors often prove to be less invasive in the running of the company and allow founders freedom to control its direction.

- Senior management role.

  Day to day control of a company resides in its management, which is empowered by its Directors, who are appointed by its shareholders. There is therefore a wide separation of powers between ownership and the daily operations of a company. A resident inventor in a senior management position may therefore have, to all intents and purposes, *de facto* control of the company and the invention, irrespective of fractional ownership of the company.

- Diversified investment base.

  The power of the shareholders resides with their ability to vote on resolutions put before General Meetings, including the confirmation of the appointment of Directors. Company founders generally retain a significant fraction of the company. By ensuring that no single investor outside of this inner circle gathers a significant fraction of equity, founders can retain control until other shareholders can act collectively.

- Financial instruments.

  Sophisticated investors do understand that as minority shareholders they are removed from the heart of power of their investee companies, and they have a number of financial instruments at their disposal to maximise their influence. These are discussed later in greater depth. In the rush to secure funding such instruments are often inaccurately viewed as secondary to the price of equity. Founders must however, negotiate these clauses with all vigour. In the rare circumstances in which they find themselves holding negotiating power, inventors and founders should, as far as possible, use these financial instruments to their own advantage. Notably the award of options (performance-related equity allocations) and anti-dilution clauses can go someway to redressing dilution.

Relinquishing Control

As the investment base broadens, and the company expands, acquiring momentum and developing its own culture, its fundamental characteristics may change. What started as an entrepreneurial and independent adventure can easily grow to become a corporation in which decision-making is ponderous, potentially losing much of its attraction to the freethinking inventor, who would literally rather be back in the shed tinkering.

The wise inventor or founder must understand the best time to leave the company to run its true course. Whilst investors may initially insist upon retaining founding expertise, this is often made redundant by the employment of professional management teams and developers. After all, the skill set and discipline of invention can differ greatly from that required for product development. The inventor intent on a graceful exit must assure this redundancy within the company, and negotiate a financial exit with existing or new shareholders. This exit need not be complete, the inventor perhaps maintaining a consulting role to the company, and a modest shareholding. The founder must not however, be cornered into a position in which he or she has a significant shareholding, but without effective control.

7.1.5
Inventive Myopia

Many inventors inevitably suffer from a form of inventive short-sightedness; their horizon is limited to development of the invention. Whilst this focus may be useful throughout the development process, it makes inventors notoriously problematic commercial partners. Inventors are encouraged therefore to understand this tendency within themselves and to reflect honestly upon their exact objectives in commercialisation of the invention. Notably a time may come when the inventor will need to exchange control of the invention for financial gain. The emotional disengagement with the invention, and its translation into a purely economic vehicle is a difficult transition.

7.2
Strategy

Chapter 2 defines the issues around patent strategy, identifies environmental and competitive determinants of patent generation, and questions the attitudes to risk displayed by the inventor. In defining corporate strategy and structure these elements are again examined, but with the addition of a key constituent – the investor. This chapter discusses the investor in various forms, and the relationship between investor and inventor. At this point, it is sufficient to introduce the investor as provider of the funds necessary to develop and commercialise the invention.

Study the books in your local business bookshop, and it is evident that numerous weighty tomes are available covering corporate strategy, and for each author there is a different emphasis. Indeed corporate strategy has seen a range of trends, from commitment to flexibility, diversification to divestment. This author has no intention of reviewing the field of corporate strategy, or indeed of recommending a particular philosophy.

The picture for the inventor is much more simple; the strategy is to leverage the invention through the market exclusivity offered by a patent, into profit. The invention must be sufficiently developed to successfully apply for a patent, but once an application is submitted a number of options are open to make money. The patent may be sold, the patent licensed to a third party, or at the extreme, a product developed employing the patent. Regardless of commercialisation route however, there is one strategic concept that is essential to the inventor; that of strategic alignment.

7.2.1
Strategic Alignment

Strategic alignment is a simple concept that dictates that all elements of the business fit into an overall corporate objective. This requires that inventor, invention, investors and employees present a coordinated front that fits with the external environment. It is only when circumstances, resources and expectations are aligned that objectives can be seamlessly achieved.

To formally ensure that this target of strategic alignment is reached, the Business Plan is a useful document. This is discussed further in the context of fundraising, but the young technology company must particularly answer the questions:

- What development and patent work needs to be performed?
- What investment of resources is required?
- To what extent is the inventor happy to relinquish control of the invention?
- Given this relationship between resources and control, to what degree should the patent be developed into a product?
- What organisation and skills are required to achieve this objective?

- What funding is required to create this organisation and to achieve its goals?

It is important that the answers to these questions fit seamlessly together and the astute reader will note a certain circularity. A degree of iteration may be required to fully answer all questions. Good strategy dictates an integrated and committed approach; that all elements of the business are aligned and the internal competences and assets of the business positioned to capture profit from the external environment.

7.2.2
Flexibility and Commitment

Strategic alignment depends upon elements of the business being aligned around a central plan, and this necessarily dictates that time and financial resources are committed to this plan, and consumed in its exercise. This commitment is at the heart of good corporate strategy, and must extend across all aspects of the organisation, however fledgling.

Commitment of resources to a plan does not however, dictate that the plan is fixed in stone, nor that resources cannot be redeployed. Indeed the plan itself can capture some of this flexibility. The young technology start-up for example, cannot know at its outset whether the stock market will favour technology fundraising in 2–3 years time. It can however, line-up the necessary data and people to support such an activity if the funding window is indeed open. It can meanwhile develop fallback funding sources and strategies.

Advocating flexibility is not to say that a company should be so flexible that a corporate alignment is hard to identify, but a certain room to manoevre permits a company to respond to changes in the external environment.

7.2.3
The Extent of Product Development

In making commercial and financial plans one key question continually revisits the technology company; to what extent should the patent be developed into a product, rather than licensed or sold? At essence lies the trade-off between the required investment and the financial return. The more development time and money is invested into an invention, turning it from invention to patent, patent to prototype, prototype to product, the greater the share of profits retained by the company. However, the longer licensing or sale is resisted, the greater the level of resources will be consumed from within the company and from its founders and investors. The key factors in determining the extent of product development are discussed below.

Resource Level

In many sectors the level of resources needed defines the extent to which product development can remain independent; the 100 m € required for development of a drug is clearly beyond most, if not all, inventors. Large companies have spent a great deal of both money and time in building the skills that are needed to develop patents through to products, and partnership is a logical way for the inventor to leverage these existing competencies.

With our relatively mature capital markets however, this reason is becoming decreasingly important, and even large sums of money are available for the determined, persuasive inventor with the right invention. Many inventors have progressed their invention all the way through to market, even in capitally intensive industry sectors. Reliance on capital markets however, dictates that a company and its owners are ready to relinquish much of their control over the company and its future, and that the technology itself is sufficiently mature to raise the level of funding required to develop and market a product. Raising funds in this way can also be immensely time-intensive, and a distraction from technical development. This said, in the context of long term planning, capital market access should not be far from the inventor's mind.

Risk, Return and Control

As has been observed, the mantra of risk, return and control goes a long way to define the boundaries within which corporate strategy must be defined. Indeed, the limits within which strategy is made can be very constricting. An inventor who wants to retain control must develop the invention for longer, and yet this requires more money and so the release of control. There is no solution to this paradox – investors, inventor and founders must have similar and realistic expectations, and a fully planned and financially modelled strategy must be agreed.

Risk and return are at the heart of the strategic decision as to how far to develop a technology before partnership. Early revenues come with limited risk, but at the expense of larger downstream sums. Late partnership, or a go-it-alone strategy is expensive but, if successful, grants greater returns, and may be preferred by inventors, founders and investors alike.

7.3
Company Formation

It goes without saying that readers need not have formed a company in order to invent, or indeed to file or be granted a patent. Before long however, it will be necessary to establish a corporate architecture around the invention or patent. This achieves several objectives:
- Investment. Investors do not generally invest in ideas, but in companies, and the formation of a company permits investors to put their capital to work in commercialising the invention. This

investment will take the form of cash or the commitment of cash, in exchange for shares in the company (known as equity) or the commitment of shares. Shares are literally the investors "share" in the company.

- Limited Liability. This legal company structure ensures that shareholders are liable for company debts only up to the value of their shareholding. If the company becomes bankrupt limited status protects shareholders from having to provide further funds. This status is generally essential to attract external funding. Whilst other Company structures do exist, such as sole proprietorship or partnerships, these do not provide this protection.
- Tax. Many jurisdictions stimulate innovation by the provision of favourable tax opportunities for start-up companies. In the UK, for example, Taper tax relief, reduces the final capital gain liability for each year that shares in a qualifying company are held. Most of these methods to legally reduce taxation are dependent upon the formation of a formal company.

Establishing a company is relatively straightforward, though in every country, several different types of company exist, each with its own benefits to the entrepreneurial inventor. Limited companies or their local equivalent, have the great advantage of sheltering the owner from liability, but other forms such as partnerships, limited partnerships, and sole trader status convey different advantages, not least of all, simplicity. Company agents can be found on the Internet or through local or national Development Agencies. These professionals can usually provide off-the-shelf or new companies. If taking an off-the-shelf company, readers should carefully check that the company is clean; that it has no debts or legacy of previous ownership.

7.3.1
Assignment of IP

Chapter 4 discusses the ownership of Intellectual Property rights, and the issues around co-invention and employment. These questions notwithstanding, it is imperative that the IP ownership is transferred to the Company, without encumbrances. It is the IP in which investors will be interested, and it must therefore belong, through the Company, to the Shareholders.

Shareholders are looking for clean undisputed IP, which belongs to the Company without complication. Outstanding employee-invention issues are likely to act as a deterrent to inward investment. Although IP assignment is a relatively straightforward execution, shareholders may insist that the Company formally warrants that the IP is owned and that there are no known barriers to this ownership. This is entirely reasonable, and if such warrants can not be made, the Company should certainly seek advice from a specialist patent agent, familiar with local regulations. Investors will also insist that future improvements and developments of the invention, along with any past or future related inventions are assigned to the Company. This too is reasonable.

Assignment documentation is simple, but should be drawn up by a lawyer. Indeed this is a good opportunity for the Company to develop a relationship with a vital member of the team. Much of the advice in Chapter 3 is relevant to the selection of a lawyer as well as a Patent Agent. Whilst legal advice can be expensive, there are pivotal moments in a Company's development that should be carefully and professionally documented. Assignment, investment, licensing and eventual sale all fall into this category.

7.3.2
Ownership Structure

Inventors, investors and advisors bring invention, money and wisdom, respectively to the start-up company. These assets are required in different measures as the company grows, and all three have a legitimate ownership claim over the company. The allocation of equity between these founders is a matter for negotiation, based on the respective contributions, expectations and positions of each party. It is very much worth recalling at this point that very little of substance has been created and yet when value is at its least tangible, the absence of financial reference points seems to make such discussions more difficult. It is critical that a young company does not get stuck in a quagmire of in-fighting, but builds strong relationships between founders and commercial and technical momentum.

This need to reach agreement should not blind inventors, in particular, to the commercial reality of equity allocation. They must ensure that they are suitably compensated for the assignment of IP, and that the resources contributed by early investors and founders are sufficient for the task in hand.

7.4
The Business Plan

Small ambitious companies seeking to commercialise a patent need to develop a business plan, and this plan serves two functions. It is one of the main tools that investors employ to evaluate the company as a potential investment, and it provides a roadmap for the company, based on rigorous professional analysis of the market, environment and economic potential for the patent. The business plan may be the first time that the inventors commercial plans come under objective and external scrutiny.

The business plan must be carefully articulated and addressed to its specific readership. As a stand-alone document it should pre-empt any questions readers may have, and convey not only the cold commercial potential of the invention, but also the passion, drive and energy of the inventor. Potential investors often receive hundreds of proposals a day, and give each only a cursory inspection. Professional, articulate and convincing presentation is essential.

Investors do understand that a business plans provides only a snapshot of a company and they will be primarily focussed on three key elements of the plan outlined in Box 9. A fourth topic, financial modelling, is discussed in greater detail in the next section in the context of valuation.

7.4.1
People

Professional investors often report that they invest primarily in people, and the plan should reflect this, emphasising the experience, skills and commitment of the team. At this stage, of course, the company may only consist of the inventor. In this case the inventor must demonstrate the commercial awareness that key additional people are required. Investors may often have networks of contacts who may be able to help.

7.4.2
Invention

As a technology-based company, the invention is key to the business plan, and should be carefully described. The plan needs to pitch this description at the right technical level; an investor is more likely to engage in an invention that can be understood. Drawings, figures and experiments are helpful in this regard. The plans for the invention need to be explored, describing the goals and costs of further Research and Development, along with the plans for patent protection.

7.4.3
Market

What is the underlying market for the invention? Revenues from the invention ultimately derive from the market, either in the form of direct sales of a product, or indirectly through partnership, in its various forms, with a company with existing products. The business plan needs to describe this market; the products that will employ the invention, the target market segments, the market positioning in terms of quality and price. For a license-based strategy the plan needs to identify and profile potential licensees, and elucidate a partnership rationale from the perspective of both companies.

Investors need to understand the competitive environment of the invention, and how this competition will be fought. They need to see that patent protection notwithstanding, the inventor has a credible commercial orientation and appetite for the marketplace.

Box 9
Business Plan Content

- Executive investment summary
- Background to the invention
- Potential customers and demand
- Sales and marketing statistics
- Competitive assessment
- Patent portfolio
- Research and development
- Product process and supply
- Plant and factory requirements
- Regulatory environment
- Backgrounds of founders and key managers
- Financial forecasts
- Magazine and newspaper articles about the company

7.5
Financial Forecasting and Valuation

The financial forecast for the invention was mentioned in Chapter 2, and throughout this book inventors are encouraged to weigh carefully the costs of product and patent development against the scale and plausibility of future profit. The business plan formally presents this balance in the form of a financial model. This model serves two functions throughout the life of the company: financial planning and valuation.

The small company must carefully plan its spending and fundraising to ensure that it continues to have the funds to support development. A company that does not have the funds to pay its employees or suppliers is bankrupt, regardless of the progress it has made and the value of its work. Careful financial planning identifies areas of cash-flow weakness and allows restitution to be made, identifies areas in which savings can be made or taxation avoided, and permits the business to understand and minimise its cost of capital. Financial planning is largely an exercise that is internal to an organisation. Valuation models, on the other hand, are often used with potential investors to understand the price of equity. For this reason, budgeting and valuation models may differ slightly – managers electing to be conservative internally and outwardly optimistic. This is to be expected, and indeed, investors themselves expect to receive optimistic forecasts. Companies must however maintain a tight control on models to ensure that they are appropriate for the purpose to which they are put.

Depending on the technology area and the competitive environment, valuation models should consider time horizons from 5–15 years, and include a terminal value. Budgeting models need to reflect monthly forecasts over a 24-month period. Models need continual review and refinement based on changes in the company and in the external market.

7.5.1
Revenue Modelling

Revenues include all forecast sources of income, including upfront payments, milestones and royalties. Where appropriate, typical industry figures should be adopted for license fees. Equity fundraising does not qualify as revenue, and is granted special treatment. A typical revenue model might outline commercially available market forecasts, identify the market share of a potential licensee, and then calculate a fraction of this revenue as a royalty payment.

Different revenue models and hence 'deal' valuations can be structured for each potential licensee, with a number of different license structures. This kind of simulation is critical in understanding the relative value of exclusive and non-exclusive partnerships, and in negotiating valuable licenses.

7.5.2
Cost Modelling

Cost modelling is essential to ensure that funds are available to meet anticipated costs, and to track the inevitable variation from the planned budget. Costs should include the expenses that the business will incur in R&D and patenting, licensing and marketing, employment, legal and advisory fees. These figures reflect the cash that the company will need to consume before attaining the self-sufficiency of profitability.

It is clearly difficult to accurately forecast the future, particularly in fast-moving technology areas. Nevertheless the financial model should build a forward-looking picture of the business; its size, scope, areas of operations. Critically the model must be internally consistent – there is no point in a cost model that promises a streamlined outsourced operation, but whose revenue is dependent on in-house manufacture. Modellers must pay particular attention to adhere to this principle and must identify the full costs consequences of decisions. For example, companies may decide to manufacture for themselves, employing a production workforce. The full cost of this workforce must include facilities, payroll staff, pension and state contributions, sick and maternity pay.

7.5.3
Net Present Value

When considering value, time and money are inextricably linked. 100 € are worth more to me now than they will be in one year. I if take the money now to a bank, they will pay interest on the money, and in one year, I will have, for example, 105 €. Overall therefore, I would rather have 100 € now, than in one year's time. Indeed, 100 € now, is perhaps the equivalent of 105 € in 12 months time.

As a company, therefore, the sooner a revenue is realised the greater its value to the company. Similarly, the later a cost is incurred, the smaller its real value. This introduces the concept of net present value, or NPV. The NPV of an organisation is the discounted total of its profits into the future (technically its free cash flow). Discounting is the process of adjusting future amounts into their value today, and depends upon the use of a figure known as the Cost of Capital. Discounting is time dependent; cash flows are adjusted for each year that they are removed from the present – an exponential process.

The cost of capital, or discount rate, is a simple concept, but one behind which lies a great deal of intricacy. Simply put, the discount rate is a measure of the level of risk to which the cashflows are exposed, and this mirrors the expected return of the organisation. High-risk cashflows are given a high discount rate; after all, their value is unlikely to materialise, whereas guaranteed cashflows (the Central Bank is effectively zero-risk in its repayments) have low discount rates, modelling inflation, rather than risk. A true Weighted Average Cost of Capital, WACC, additionally models the source of funding, with debt funding bearing a lower cost than equity.

Box 10

	2005	2006	2007	2008	2009	2010	2011	2012	2013	2014
Revenue / $m										
Licensee market forecast			5.00	10.00	25.00	50.00	50.00	50.00	25.00	10.00
Upfront payment	0.25									
Prototype milestone		0.50								
Launch milestone			1.00							
Royalty of 5%			0.25	0.50	1.25	2.50	2.50	2.50	1.25	0.50
Manufacturing revenue			0.60	1.20	3.00	6.00	6.00	6.00	3.00	1.20
Total gross revenue	0.25	0.50	1.85	1.70	4.25	8.50	8.50	8.50	4.25	1.70
Expenses / $m										
Research and development	0.10	0.25	0.50							
Business development	0.25	0.25	0.25							
Manufacturing		0.50	1.00	2.50	5.00	5.00	5.00	2.50	1.00	0.00
Patent costs	0.10	0.25	0.10	0.05	0.05	0.05	0.05	0.05	0.05	0.05
Administration, legal, general	0.01	0.03	0.09	0.09	0.21	0.43	0.43	0.43	0.21	0.09
Total expenses	0.46	1.28	1.94	2.64	5.26	5.48	5.48	2.98	1.26	0.14
Revenue-Expenses / $m	-0.21	-0.78	-0.09	-0.94	-1.01	3.03	3.03	5.53	2.99	1.57

Company discount rate	15%

Net present value-80$m	3.62

Box 10 highlights a simple NPV calculation for a technology start-up. The NPV calculation is essential in determining the value of an organisation or a project. Indeed including a time value of money, and adjusting for risk, can highlight that an invention or patent is not worth pursuing. As has been emphasised elsewhere, it is important to pay heed to such models – they are the formal statement that the costs do not match the plausibility (risk) of the return.

7.5.4
Real-World Valuation

Many economists would agree that the true value of a company is its NPV. Nevertheless, in the real world, there are a myriad of methods used to value companies. Many of these methods are dated and have been shown to be inaccurate, but remain popular even with the professional investment community. Entrepreneurs must not be surprised to see their companies valued by a range of esoteric methods by investors;

Payback Period
Payback is the bluntest of valuation tools. The payback period of an investment is the number of years it takes before cumulative cashflows equal the initial investment. A short payback is interpreted as a good investment. This method makes no allowance for the time value of money, and totally ignores all revenues occurring after the payback. Technology companies are particularly poorly valued by this method – investments tend to be long-term, risky and with very high relative payouts. Avoid investors who rely on this method!

Internal Rate of Return
IRR is a widely employed valuation method, which if used accurately is not fundamentally flawed. Its criticism is simply that it is unwieldy to use, and if used inaccurately leads to poor valuation and investment decisions. At heart the IRR is the discount rate that would have to be used in a discounted cashflow calculation to arrive at NPV=0. Investors then compare this IRR against comparable industry or internal expectations.

Book Rate of Return
In various forms, this is a very common method of company valuation, despite suffering from inherent circularity, a collective approach, and a failure to fully adjust for time. To calculate the average book rate of return, the average profit of the company, adjusted for depreciation and taxes, is divided by the average book value of the investment, amortised over the forecast period. This ratio is then compared to some external standard, normally based on other companies in the sector, or on other investment opportunities that are available.

Price-earnings Ratio

The PER is an everyday investment term, and reflects the relationship between share price and the earnings of a company. Share price, as a measure of company value is based on the forecast value of future earnings. A high P/E ratio therefore suggests that investors believe that a company will have strong earnings growth. Companies in the same sector tend to have similar profitability, risks and growth opportunities and hence P/E ratios. By multiplying the forecast earnings of a company by the P/E ratio of comparable companies, one arrives at a valuation for the company at the point of the earnings forecast. By discounting back to the present, a current valuation for the company or technology is achieved.

The key to such real-world valuation methods is to put them in the context of NPV and to be armed with a well-conducted model from which to firmly negotiate.

7.6
Financing the Venture

Of the two forms of funding, debt and equity, debt is largely unavailable to the technology start-up company. Based on interest repayments, it is more suited to fund the expansion of existing businesses than the all-or-nothing risk of technology companies. As a consequence the majority of such companies start by using founders own savings and manage with relatively little capital.

7.6.1
Start-up Funding

Indeed the initial equity capital of start-up companies traditionally comes from the 4Fs – founders, family, friends and foolhardy investors. The budding inventor may need to tap into this network of investors to fund initial development work and patent application. The skills of this group should also not be overlooked; the business at this time operates very much on a hand-to-mouth basis, and relies on personal networks for funding and resources. The founder may have a full-time job apart from invention.

The goal of this early phase is to technically develop the invention, and to understand the market potential for the invention, to be in a position to file a patent, or indeed to have already filed. This provides the credibility to move forward to more formal investment networks.

7.6.2
Angel Investors

Entrepreneurs looking to raise less than 400,000 € in high risk early-stage funding are likely to be more successful in the angel investment network than in the formal Venture Capital (VC) market. Angels are high net-worth individuals, prepared to invest both their capital and experience in start-up businesses. Though angel networks have a lower profile than their VC counterparts, they invest $10–20bn per year in the USA alone.

Angel investors tend to invest less than 80,000 € each per investment, though co-investing and syndication is possible for larger sums. This funding is granted in exchange for equity, held over a relatively long period. Investors would normally seek exit within five years, and expect a return on their investment of the order of 30% per year in start-up companies. This return is not greatly different from that expected by VCs, and angels do not earn their name, or indeed their wings, because of the price paid for the equity. Angels are so-called because their investment criteria are often less proscriptive than VCs. Without investors of their own to answer to, they tend to be relatively quick to make investment decisions, to take more generous horizons, and to impose fewer limitations on management behaviour.

Angels, frequently successful self-made businesspeople are often motivated by factors beyond money, and take pleasure from taking an involved role in their investments. The company benefits from the experience and network of the investor, as well as the money.

Identifying angel investors is a matter of following local and industry networks, as well as contacts made through family and friends and alumni and professional networks. Investors themselves use similar networks of business relationships, including bankers, lawyers and accountants to identify opportunities. Local investors may be accessible through regional development agencies, or may indeed be prominent members of the local community. Successful high-profile entrepreneurs within the industry of the invention represent a good opportunity to access the subterranean networks within the sector. Often these people will be familiar to the inventor, even if not known personally.

Formal angel networks seek to act as intermediaries between investors and opportunities. They can be useful in making introductions, but the scale of charges should be identified before their use. Some make only nominal fees and are underwritten by governmental agencies, whilst others charge significant percentage-based introductory fees and should be avoided.

7.6.3
Venture Capital

The public profile of VC investors is high relative to the number of investments that they make. Funded by investors of their own, VCs back a portfolio of small high-risk, high-growth companies, usually looking to exit their money through sale of the company within five to seven years. VCs seek to make an annual return on their investment of up to 80%, depending on the stage of the investment.

Indeed to control the level of risk to which their capital is exposed VCs generally stage their investments over a number of tranches or rounds. This enables them to allocate part of their funds only if product development proceeds successfully. This de-risking also works in the favour of the company, which needs to grant fewer shares to raise the same funds, as outlined in Table 7.1. In the example by staging VC investments IA and IB over two tranches, the company issues 2m shares, rather than the 3m it would have had to sell if it had tried to raise £ 3m in the 1A funding round.

Tab. 7.1 Simplified illustration of successive funding rounds.

Event	Total equity raised	Total authorised shares	Sub- scription price	Shares issued	Valuation	Ownership of inventor	Value of inventors stake
Incorporation	£ 1	100	1p	100	£ 1	100%	£ 1
Funding from financial founder/ shares rebased in value	£ 100k	2 m	10p	1999k	£ 200,000	50%	£ 100 k
VC IA	£ 1.5m	3.5 m	£ 1	1.5 m	£ 3.5 m	28.5 %	£ 1 m
VC IB	£ 1.5m	4.0 m	£ 3	0.5 m	£ 12 m	25 %	£ 3 m
VC II	£ 6 m	5.0 m	£ 6	1.0 m	£ 30 m	20 %	£ 6 m

In managing to secure VC funding, a start-up takes a huge leap forward, and accesses, albeit it at a price, the resources to commercialise its technology. In fact, the price reflected purely in equity may not be either unreasonable or onerous. VCs do however have a myriad of ways to lower the risk of their investment, and a typical investment may use relatively complex instruments to achieve this. The use of Convertible Preferred Shares grants VCs specific rights compared with holders of common shares. Add to these, dividend rights, redemption rights, registration rights, recapitalization rights, approval rights, rights to appoint directors and one can see how deals with VCs can take up to six months to complete (and how angels suddenly seem angelic). Often VCs also negotiate restrictions on management behaviour, including salary levels, life insurance, non-compete agreements and restrict current shareholders from selling their stock to third parties, or from leaving the company.

7.6.4
Shareholder Structures and Agreement

An inventor will not be able to proceed for long down a commercial path without being faced with the seemingly daunting task of establishing the Articles of Association and Shareholders Agreement for the company. The Articles of a company outline the purpose and intentions of the company, and the methods that will be used to achieve this goal. The Shareholders Agreement regulates the ways in which the shareholders relate to the company, including specifics of voting rights and changes in control. If one imagines the company as a house, owned by a great number of investors, for example, it is clear that some structure must be established to regulate the way in which the house is used, if it is to be extended, or sold.

Whilst different countries have their own particular versions of these documents, and their own legal requirements, these documents are largely at the discretion of the company. The agreement is effectively a contract with shareholders, and depending on the investors, may be the source of intense negotiation. At each round of funding it is likely that the Shareholder's Agreement will be renegotiated, and with each successive rewrite the document can become increasingly complex. There is little value in detailed and protracted contracting between founding investors. Instead, the inventor is encouraged in early funding to generate a simple document, covering how the company will be run, who has day-to-day running, how new equity can be released, and the basis for appointing and removing Directors. Care should be taken to identify what happens if an equity-owning founder decides to leave the company.

In subsequent discussions with professional investors, founders should seek formal legal advice, and pay particular attention not only to the price at which equity issued, but also to the terms and conditions with which this occurs.

7.6.5
Working With Investors

Investors invest in people. They are however, rational and economic and certainly in the case of VCs, have investors of their own, to whom they answer, targets to meet and salaries and bonuses to make. The relationship between inventor and investor is therefore a unique and delicately balanced one. On one hand investors are well connected and skilled and dedicated assets of the company. On the other, they are driven by their own profit.

Fundamentally investors are financially and psychologically rewarded by the success of their investments and will leverage their networks of contacts to help achieve this success. This is one of the reasons why well-connected and experienced investors are invaluable to the start-up company. A continual dialogue with investors will maintain strong and open communications, with issues identified and addressed early, opportunities captured, and development accelerated. Good managers understand that shareholders own the company, and hence the patents, products and inventions. Inventors, understandably reluctant to lose ownership and control of their creations and must continually reappraise the situation in which they find themselves.

Whilst the goals of both investors and founders are generally aligned in the desire to maximise profit through product development, there are inevitable differences that emerge, reflecting disparities in attitude to risk, return and timing. It is in anticipation of these differences that shareholder agreements are drawn up in such detail, and that VCs insist upon sophisticated investment vehicles. There is certainly no formula to define how best to manage this relation. The key is to understand the principle; that at heart, the objective of value creation is shared, but that investors have their own financial ambitions. Founders and inventors must understand their own attitude to risk and their expected return from the company, and negotiate to achieve this position.

7.7
Negotiation

It is beyond the scope of this volume to present a detailed account of negotiation methods and techniques. Indeed, recent years have seen an expansion in the practical and academic study of this discipline. Negotiation is central to the creation and the retention of value by the inventor, and so some discussion is highly relevant. What is presented here is a single simple framework, which is independent of personal characteristics, and one that can be broadly applied in all settings.

BATNA

Imagine walking into a meeting with a leading VC company. You have tried numerous other investors, without success. Imagine now that you are walking into the same meeting, but that earlier in the morning you agreed terms with a different investor, and the document, as yet unsigned, is sitting snugly in your breast pocket. The two conversations will be very different. In the second scenario you have a strong BATNA – a Best Alternative to a Negotiated Agreement. If discussions fail, this is the fallback position. A strong fallback grants power in a discussion, whereas a weak, or absent BATNA forces a negotiator to accept what is offered.

Whilst strong analytical and communication skills and the ability to form open, resilient relationships are useful personal qualities in a negotiation, what creates power is BATNA. The negotiator who creates a strong BATNA is greatly empowered, even if this is relatively poorly communicated.

Strengthening the BATNA

Each organisation comprises a number of internal and external relationships, and to a lesser or greater degree these relationships impact on one another to form an extended network. These can be mapped to form a picture of the company, and of the importance of any single relationship. The negotiating position of the inventor discussed above would be strengthened by lining up an alternative deal, but also by a number of other factors; personal circumstances, a license already negotiated, by having a comprehensive supply chain. In each case the factors make walking away without settlement a more palatable event, and remove barriers to completing a deal. Through the creative extension of these multilateral relationship networks, and their leverage across negotiations, a company acts to reduce its dependence upon, and therefore improve the BATNA of, any single negotiation.

For a negotiation to reach a successful conclusion, a zone of potential agreement (ZOPA) must exist between the BATNAs of the two parties, between what one party is prepared to pay and the other party is prepared to accept. By improving the BATNA the negotiator narrows the zone towards the other party. The exact of point of agreement within the ZOPA is a distributive function and one that is dependent on a number of factors, including perceptions of relative strengths and negotiation technique. The network approach of improving the BATNA allows even novice negotiators to reach strong settlements with highly experienced counterparts.

Indeed, the inventor in negotiations with financiers and investors is very likely to be at a distinct disadvantage. Professional investors have a refined negotiation technique based on repeated practical learning. The start-up company will complete perhaps three funding rounds over its lifetime. Yet by opening up a network of alternatives and consciously improving the BATNA these odds can be substantially redressed. The art of negotiation is in communicating this power in a manner that is depersonalised and yet which builds upon the personal relationship between the parties.

Through extensive financial planning and modelling and by aligning the organisation around a clear strategic vision, the negotiating position is inherently improved. The organisation has a momentum and direction, planned flexibility, and sufficient time to achieve its goals and can therefore withstand the failure of any single negotiation.

8
The Importance of Business Structures to the Exploitation of IP

Christoph Regierer

The authors of this book have emphasised that patents should be considered not simply from their technical aspects, but also within a comprehensive economic context. For example, the chapters on licensing and start-up structures make it clear that technical, legal and economic aspects of IP need to be considered in a coordinated manner. This chapter will contribute to this integrated approach by outlining the business structures and accounting principles that support the capture of value from intellectual property.

As a consequence of their nature, patents and other IP are treated differently under corporate and tax law. The law makes a general distinction between tangible and intangible assets. Tangible assets are, as the name suggests, objects such as real property, buildings, machines, motor vehicles and office equipment. As a general rule, tangible assets can be consumed, damaged or reduced by use.

By contrast, intangible assets, lack physical characteristics. Rights such as patents, know-how and technical processes are intangible assets that remain unchanged by use and retain this characteristic even when electronically stored or bound in chemical substances. Although this physical form is tangible, the underlying asset remains intangible. This separation of the physical form and the intangible content defines this asset class.

The lack of physical characteristics allows intangible assets, such as patents, to be detached from their operational context and to be separately valued, sold, and licensed. Indeed, the recognition that intangible assets can be separated from the operational process and used as independent assets greatly expands the economic potential and value of an enterprise. Companies are adopting evermore sophisticated structures to better exploit the dichotomy between operational functions and intangible assets, and this is reflected in the way in which enterprises are legally structured, present their accounts, and report their financial results. Consequently, the regulatory framework of these financial activities also continues to evolve. This chapter addresses several of the issues that arise from the intangible nature of patents as business assets.

8.1
Legal Forms of Transferring IP Ownership

The question of the legal form of IP ownership was discussed in the chapter on structuring and financing start-ups. There it was outlined that cooperation with financial investors is dependant on the company having formally structured rights to IP. This chapter discusses methods of transferring ownership interests in IP.

The merger of know-how entrepreneurs and financial investors into a common enterprise not only serves to secure the interests of all parties in the IP, and thus ultimately securing commercial success. The enterprise also represents an independent legal entity that controls the future of the IP. The start-up company, for example, will be the object of financing, such as bank loans, shareholder loans and other forms of hybrid financing. It is an employer, a tax subject, and is required to obtain permits and other similar authorisations. If the project fails and perhaps along with it the enterprise, all IP remains within the company and does not revert back to the initial inventor. The contributed IP is an asset owned by the start-up and must be disposed of in accordance with corporate, tax and insolvency law.

Company start-up and IP transfer represent major crossroads in IP ownership, and need to be navigated carefully. Most often the patent owner is a natural person, and the start-up company is a distinct legal entity. Consequently, the transfer of the patent from private ownership into corporate ownership requires a formal act. This transfer should be structured in accordance with the interests of the parties. The following are typical ownership configurations:

- Transfer as a capital contribution-in-kind
  The typical start-up configuration structures the distribution of shares between the patent owner (know-how entrepreneur) and the financial investors. The know-how entrepreneur and financial investor will appraise the value of the patent and thereupon negotiate their respective share ratios. The IP often represents the only, or perhaps the most important, instrument for raising capital on the part of the know-how entrepreneur. Therefore, from his point of view, a transfer is worthwhile if it raises the necessary capital from financial investors and is structured as a capital contribution-in-kind at current fair value. The patent owner exchanges rights in the patent for shares in the company. Typically, he will continue to develop the idea within the new company and this assures that the shares are retained by investors and that they increase in value.

  A problem arises in determining fair value when the patent or know how has not yet been commercially exploited. It then becomes necessary to determine a value without having reference to a market price. Theoretically, the following three methods are available:

- The "cost approach" attempts to determine what costs would be incurred to produce an identical asset. When valuing unexploited patents, costs include patent attorney costs, registration fees as well as the personnel and material costs necessary for its production. In practice, these costs can hardly be estimated because patent development is a complex and highly integrated process. Therefore, the cost approach is not particularly useful for patents developed in new technology areas.
- The "market approach", which makes its valuation based on the market price of comparable assets, is also not normally suited for innovative patents. The reason is obvious: For innovative technologies there are generally no comparable patents or products from which a market price could be determined.
- Therefore, an "income-based approach" has developed in which the value of an intangible asset is derived from its potential future revenues. This naturally requires a determination of future revenues. The method most often used to make this determination is called the "relief from royalties method". This method examines the savings on licensing fees which may result from ownership of the patent. The advantage of this method is that the market now provides adequate information on the value of royalties which would allow for estimation. For this reason the "relief from royalties method" is commonly used to measure the value of patents owned by start-ups.

- Transfer by licensing
  If the patent owner is not in the typical start-up situation, a complete transfer of all patent rights may not be required, and a license transaction may suffice. This is the case when the patent is not fundamental to the licensee, but is nevertheless beneficial for technical reasons, or if the patent owner is in such a strong negotiating position that he is not compelled to completely dispose of the patent, and is able to separate use from ownership. Such a license may be exclusive or non-exclusive, and may be structured financially as discussed in Chapter 6, to include upfront, milestone and royalty fees. Licensing may be preceded by a transfer of the patent to an independent company which itself has the purpose of managing the licensing of the patent. Patent administration companies are often located in advantageous tax jurisdictions.
- Transfer by sale
  Outright sale of IP is an option distinct from a transfer by contribution-in-kind, or through licensing. The sale results in a transfer

of the patent to the purchasing entity and the owner of the patent will receive the purchase price, with or without encumbrances. For example, non-expert financial investors may not be interested in the IP without the continuing services of the inventor, whereas established enterprises may well have the opposite interest: attaining full ownership of a patent without any future involvement of the original owner. In a transfer by sale the question arises whether remuneration is structured as cash or equity, or both.

The above examples make clear that the legal relationship between the know-how entrepreneur and the patent-developing company can be organised in different ways. The structure selected is dependant upon the respective needs of the inventor and financial investor with regard to risk, return and control, as well as the legal and tax structures available in the respective jurisdiction. Therefore, it is important for the parties hoping to exploit the patent to carefully reflect on their legal options. From the view point of the know-how entrepreneur, it is recommendable that he familiarise himself with the available legal structures in advance. An advisor may be helpful prior to contacting financial investors. It is important for the know-how entrepreneur to develop an independent concept of the value of the patent as well as how the concept can be convincingly presented so as to have an optimal negotiating position when talking to financial investors. This is of particular importance because the interest of financial investors in having a patent brought into a new venture will be increased by the greater value of the patent. It is therefore in the patent owner's interest to devote a considerable amount of time in developing a value concept for the patent.

8.2
Intellectual Property and Financial Reporting

Patents and other IP, together with the knowledge acquired through associated research and development, are the most significant assets of technology companies. The question of how these assets are shown in the company's financial accounting is important. In all corporate transactions, such as capital increases within the scope of new financing, asset or share deals within a profit-taking strategy, or management buy-outs, financial statements provide financial information to owners, management, employees, banks and investors. The presentation of these statements, particularly with regard to the valuation of intangible assets, is undergoing considerable change at present. This is particularly true in the EU, where a transformation to IAS/IFRS accounting standards is underway.

Earlier EU accounting guidelines did not permit companies to show intangible assets on the balance sheet. The result was that all costs incurred in creating these assets, in particular personnel, office leasing and raw materials, were treated as current operating expenses. Without corresponding revenues, technology companies found themselves operating at a dramatic loss in the start-up years. As a consequence, typically, these companies were characterised by the fact that the book value of their share capital, as reflected in their accounts, was considerably below the market value as reflected by their share price.

Although research costs may not be capitalised under IAS/IFRS standards, development costs may be capitalised when they satisfy defined conditions – e.g. technical feasibility, availability of the resources necessary to realise a profit, and reliable determinability of the corresponding production costs. In other words, the development of new processes, systems, services or products based on a patent will increasingly appear in company balance sheets as assets. As a direct result, the market value and book value of technology companies will converge.

The personal and institutional use of the financial statements of technology companies will have to adjust to these changes. Typical situations in which new accounting standards make a difference are:

- Performance-based transactions:
  It is not unusual for transactions to be made dependent upon financial results. This might include milestone payments within the scope of financing, compensation for hybrid financing structures or remuneration for management and employees. It is strongly recommended that prior to agreeing to performance-based structures, the parties carefully define the accounting standards that determine performance.

- Financial planning:
  Key financial and investment decisions within technology companies are made in accordance with a financial plan. This plan includes financial reporting, equity/debt ratios, and development costs. Should the implementation of an IAS/IFRS based accounting system be required or preferred an effective cost and activity accounting, showing project-based production costs is necessary. In the absence of strong management accounting systems, the criteria for capitalising expenses cannot be met and financial plans and the decisions that depend upon them will not be accurate. Financial planning cannot be separated from the underlying management accounting.

- Consequences of capitalising intangible asset:
  Beyond the initial capitalisation of development costs, consideration must be given to the consequences of capitalisation for future financial accounting. Upon the conclusion of development and the attainment of series production capability, intangible assets must be amortised. Had the development costs not been capitalised, they would have been expensed at the time they were incurred, and thus IAS/IFRS results in a shifting of costs to later periods. In addition, IAS/IFRS requires that capitalised assets in development be subjected to a so-called "impairment test". Based on business valuation principals, this test determines whether

the anticipated future use corresponds to the current book value.
This is a complex procedure and implementation requires detailed preparation within the firm's financial system.

It is apparent that financial accounting questions have increasing importance for IP exploitation. This development is driven by the transition to IAS/IFRS, which offers companies significantly greater leeway in accounting for intangible assets. Accounting decisions have great relevance for all contracts that make reference to data from the financial reporting.

Independent of the individual questions concerning accounting for intellectual property are questions faced by every company regarding its accounting system. There is no single system solution for all companies. However, it can be said that the importance of the accounting system is regularly misjudged by technology companies. This is somewhat understandable in light of their focus on science and not on business.

If several inventors or scientists have come together in a company to work on a patent or idea, and no financial investors are associated with the company, the accounting system has the function of informing shareholders and managers of the financial situation and statutory requirements (tax office, other public offices). If no more than 10 to 15 persons are active in a company, consideration should be given to engaging an accountant to perform the bookkeeping and prepare the financial statements in order to free-up internal personnel. Regular meetings should take place with the accountant, at the very least once each quarter, in order to inform management of the current financial and liquidity status. Together with an accountant, a functional accounting and reporting system can be developed which will, in time, evolve into a customised accounting system. Upon further growth of personnel, thought can be given to in-sourcing some elements of accounting. An example of a functional division of activities would be to retain the financial accounting within the company and to have the accountant continue preparing the payroll accounts and the financial statements.

Additional questions arise when the start-up company has financial investors from the very beginning. The ability of the company to provide financial investors with informative reporting is a significant element of the accounting system. This ability is a soft fact in the valuation of the company by third-parties and should be taken seriously.

If only limited personnel capacity is valuable, the accounting function should be outsourced. However, in consideration of the increased reporting requirements for financial investors, an even earlier in-sourcing of certain accounting activities should be considered. An important element of any in-sourcing considerations would be the hard and software. Parallel to in-sourcing accounting functions, it is always recommendable to consider implementing ERP software with its budgeting and comparative cost accounting capabilities. In addition, this software should be capable of working with both the local GAAP and international accounting standards.

8.3
Tax Aspects

The scope of this book does not allow for treatment of all tax questions that arise in association with patents and other IP. Only basic questions will be addressed to clarify fundamental considerations, and to introduce the key topics for discussion with a professional tax advisor. When discussing taxes, the initial consideration is to examine the tax base and rate, at the level of both the company and of the shareholder.

8.3.1
Tax Considerations on the Company Level

From the tax perspective of the company, it is important that the costs of patent and know-how development are deductible from the taxable base. When using IAS/IFRS accounting, the commercial balance sheet and the tax balance sheet will show different results. For example, according to IAS/IFRS product development costs must be capitalised over time as an intangible asset, but tax law prohibits capitalisation and thus creates an immediate expense which reduces profits, or generates losses carried-forward. It currently cannot be said whether the cost deferring IAS/IFRS accounting standards will be used to determine taxable income in the future.

Of significant importance to the structuring of the tax base are the tax breaks available in many countries to companies involved in research and development. This issue was already touched upon in the chapter on start-up financing. These tax breaks are often structured differently depending on the jurisdiction. Some tax jurisdictions allow tax-free public subsidies, with the result that the tax base is not increased, whereas other jurisdictions allow for advantageous depreciation or allowances. Technology companies may seek to take advantage of the legal and tax structures of jurisdictions that have advantageous tax systems by establishing subsidiaries or establishing a presence in those jurisdictions. However, all countries make an effort to grant tax advantages only to those companies that intend to permanently conduct their research and development activities in that country.

The same reasoning applies to the selection of the business location based on tax rates. Many countries accept a change in business site only when the business activity itself is shifted. As a result of international competition to attract technology companies, interesting tax advantages are available both with regard to the tax base and tax rates. Nevertheless, technology companies in the development stage are subject to natural limits set by the proximity of universities, the availability of qualified employees and access to technical resources.

Typically, tax aspects are not controlling for the initial decisions on the start-up location and the organisation of the company. If however, there is an option to make use of favourable tax systems by selecting the company site, careful and structured planning is necessary. Inventors, company founders and financial investors should review the tax advantages available in the countries under consideration prior to founding the company. The tax advantages should be considered in regard to anticipated company development. If the company plan anticipates high development expenses over several years and therefore only losses are expected, and thus no tax burden exists, then systems which provide tax relief or tax credits provide no advantage. In such cases, countries are preferable that allow for tax free public subsidies as, for example, for research personnel. The opposite situation would result if, from the time the company is founded, it is clear that a profit can be anticipated as the result of exploitation or development subsidies. Clearly, a requirement for serious tax planning is long-term corporate planning. Without a long-term plan, the desired tax effects may be partially or completely lost.

After finding a suitable location from a tax point of view, importance should be placed on the practical implementation of the structural advantages offered by the location. Financial and personnel accounting, annual financial statements and tax declarations must be prepared in conformity with the laws of the country where the company is located. Local consultants need to be found.

Even though start-up companies generally do not consider changing sites for tax reasons with increasing corporate maturity this topic gains significance. For example in international joint ventures or cooperation agreements with foreign sales partners, an awareness of overseas business and tax advantages will grow.

8.3.2
Tax Considerations on the Shareholder Level

The same taxation considerations apply to the needs of shareholders as apply to the enterprise itself. Here again, the overall tax burden is determined by the tax base and tax rates. When a patent is used by a company and the former patent owner works in the company, two typical taxation situations arise; often the know-how entrepreneur has a senior managerial position within the start-up, and receives compensation corresponding to the position. Additionally, as a shareholder a taxable event occurs when shares of the start-up are sold at a profit. The capital gains tax applied to the sale of shares varies according to the jurisdiction. Although it is difficult to estimate future profits when a patent is in an early development stage, measures to reduce future tax should be considered early on. Under German law, for example, it is advantageous for managers to own shares in their start-ups through asset holding companies.

9
List of Annexes

For updates for the most recent treaties and their member states see
www.wipo.int/treaties/en

Annex 1 Paris Convention for the Protection of Industrial Property
Annex 2 PCT Contracting States
Annex 3 EPO member states and extension states
Annex 4 Nice Classification of goods and services
Annex 5 International Classification for Industrial Designs under the Locarno
Agreement
Annex 6 European Community Member States
Annex 7 Member countries of the Madrid Agreement and Madrid Protocol
Annex 8 ARIPO member states
Annex 9 OAPI member states
Annex 10 Country Codes

Intellectual Property Management. Claas Junghans, Adam Levy
Copyright © 2006 WILEY-VCH Verlag GmbH & Co. KGaA, Weinheim

Annex 1
Paris Convention for the Protection of Industrial Property (January 3rd, 2005)

The Paris Convention is the oldest international treaty still in force; for the applicant the most relevant article in practical terms will be the 4th, regulating the terms of priority for patents, trademarks, design protection and other forms of IP.

Note that under the PCT, the most relevant international treaty for patents, a priority can be used not only from any Paris Convention member state, but also from any World Trade Agreement member state.

Albania	Costa Rica
Algeria	Côte d'Ivoire
Andorra	Croatia
Antigua and Barbuda	Cuba
Argentina	Cyprus
Armenia	Czech Republic
Australia	Democratic People's Republic of Korea
Austria	Democratic Republic of the Congo
Azerbaijan	Denmark
Bahamas	Djibouti
Bahrain	Dominica
Bangladesh	Dominican Republic
Barbados	Ecuador
Belarus	Egypt
Belgium	El Salvador
Belize	Equatorial Guinea
Benin	Estonia
Bhutan	Finland
Bolivia	France
Bosnia and Herzegovina	Gabon
Botswana	Gambia
Brazil	Georgia
Bulgaria	Germany
Burkina Faso	Ghana
Burundi	Greece
Cambodia	Grenada
Cameroon	Guatemala
Canada	Guinea
Central African Republic	Guinea-Bissau
Chad	Guyana
Chile	Haiti
China	Holy See
Colombia	Honduras
Comoros	Hungary
Congo	Iceland

India

Indonesia

Iran (Islamic Republic of)

Iraq

Ireland

Israel

Italy

Jamaica

Japan

Jordan

Kazakhstan

Kenya

Kyrgyzstan

Lao People's Democratic Republic

Latvia

Lebanon

Lesotho

Liberia

Libyan Arab Jamahiriya

Liechtenstein

Lithuania

Luxembourg

Madagascar

Malawi

Malaysia

Mali

Malta

Mauritania

Mauritius

Mexico

Monaco

Mongolia

Morocco

Mozambique

Namibia

Nepal

Netherlands

New Zealand

Nicaragua

Niger

Nigeria

Norway

Oman

Pakistan

Panama

Papua New Guinea

Paraguay

Peru

Philippines

Poland

Portugal

Qatar

Republic of Korea

Republic of Moldova

Romania

Russian Federation

Rwanda

Saint Kitts and Nevis

Saint Lucia

Saint Vincent and the Grenadines

San Marino

Sao Tome and Principe

Saudi Arabia

Senegal

Serbia and Montenegro

Seychelles

Sierra Leone

Singapore

Slovakia

Slovenia

South Africa

Spain

Sri Lanka

Sudan

Suriname

Swaziland

Sweden

Switzerland

Syrian Arab Republic

Tajikistan

The former Yugoslav Republic of Macedonia

Togo

Tonga

Trinidad and Tobago

Tunisia

Turkey

Turkmenistan

Uganda

Ukraine

United Arab Emirates

United Kingdom

United Republic of Tanzania

United States of America

Uruguay

Uzbekistan

Venezuela

Viet Nam

Zambia

Zimbabwe

Annex 2

PCT Contracting States (as of July 7th, 2005)

Applying for a patent under the PCT, either directly to the World Intellectual Property Organisation (WIPO) or through national or regional patent offices, has the same effect as filing individually in each PCT member state. The PCT however does not grant patents; the applications are further processed by national or regional offices after entering the "national phase", typically after 30 months.

A preliminary examination can be requested under the PCT that gives the applicant valuable information about the chances of receiving a granted patent in the national phase.

A total of 126 states has ratified the PCT. Again, the date of ratification determines whether a PCT application included the respective country. The 30-month period to start the national phase is valid for most but not all PCT member states. Few jurisdictions have extended this period to 31 months.

AL	Albania	CO	Colombia
DZ2	Algeria	KM	Comoros
AG	Antigua and Barbuda	CG	Congo
AM2	Armenia	CR	Costa Rica
AU	Australia	CI	Côte d'Ivoire
AT	Austria	HR	Croatia
AZ	Azerbaijan	CU	Cuba
BB	Barbados	CY	Cyprus
BY	Belarus	C	Czech Republic
BE	Belgium	KP	Democratic People's Republic
BZ	Belize		of Korea
BJ	Benin	DK	Denmark
BA	Bosnia and Herzegovina	DM	Dominica
BW	Botswana	EC	Ecuador
BR	Brazil	EG	Egypt
BG	Bulgaria	GQ	Equatorial Guinea
BF	Burkina Faso	EE	Estonia
CM	Cameroon	FI	Finland
CA	Canada	FR	France
CF	Central African Republic	GA	Gabon
TD	Chad	GM	Gambia
CN	China	GE	Georgia

DE	Germany
GH	Ghana
GR	Greece
GD	Grenada
GN	Guinea
GW	Guinea-Bissau
HU	Hungary
IS	Iceland
IN	India
ID	Indonesia
IE	Ireland
IL	Israel
IT	Italy
JP	Japan
KZ	Kazakhstan
KE	Kenya
KG	Kyrgyzstan
LV	Latvia
LS	Lesotho
LR	Liberia
LY	Libyan Arab Jamahiriya (Becomes member on September 15th, 2005)
LI	Liechtenstein
LT	Lithuania
LU	Luxembourg
MG	Madagascar
MW	Malawi
ML	Mali
MR	Mauritania
MX	Mexico
MC	Monaco
MN	Mongolia
MA	Morocco
MZ	Mozambique
NA	Namibia
NL	Netherlands
NZ	New Zealand
NI	Nicaragua
NE	Niger
NG	Nigeria
NO	Norway
OM	Oman
PG	Papua New Guinea

PH	Philippines
PL	Poland
PT	Portugal
KR	Republic of Korea
MD	Republic of Moldova
RO	Romania
RU	Russian Federation
LC	Saint Lucia
VC	Saint Vincent and the Grenadines
SM	San Marino
SN	Senegal
YU	Serbia and Montenegro
SC	Seychelles
SL	Sierra Leone
SG	Singapore
SK	Slovakia
SI	Slovenia
ZA	South Africa
ES	Spain
LK	Sri Lanka
SD	Sudan
SZ	Swaziland
SE3	Sweden
CH	Switzerland
SY	Syrian Arab Republic
TJ2	Tajikistan
MK	The former Yugoslav Republic of Macedonia
TG	Togo
TT	Trinidad and Tobago
TN	Tunisia
TR	Turkey
TM	Turkmenistan
UG	Uganda
UA	Ukraine
AE	United Arab Emirates
GB	United Kingdom
TZ	United Republic of Tanzania
US	United States of America
UZ	Uzbekistan
VN	Viet Nam
ZM	Zambia
ZW	Zimbabwe

PCT Contracting States for which a Regional Patent can be Obtained via the PCT (as of November 1st, 2004)

AP ARIPO patent	BW	Botswana
	GH	Ghana
	GM	Gambia
	KE	Kenya
	LS	Lesotho
	MW	Malawi
	MZ	Mozambique
	NA	Namibia
	SD	Sudan
	SL	Sierra Leone
	SZ	Swaziland
	TZ	United Republic of Tanzania
	UG	Uganda
	ZM	Zambia
	ZW	Zimbabwe
EA Eurasian patent	AM	Armenia
	AZ	Azerbaijan
	BY	Belarus
	KG	Kyrgyzstan
	KZ	Kazakhstan
	MD	Republic of Moldova
	RU	Russian Federation
	TJ	Tajikistan
	TM	Turkmenistan
EP European patent		See below
OA OAPI patent	BF	Burkina Faso
	BJ	Benin
	CF	Central African Republic
	CG	Congo
	CI	Côte d'Ivoire
	CM	Cameroon
	GA	Gabon
	GN	Guinea
	GQ	Equatorial Guinea
	GW	Guinea-Bissau
	ML	Mali
	MR	Mauritania
	NE	Niger
	SN	Senegal

For updates see www.wipo.int/pct/en/access/legal_text.htm

Annex 3
EPO member states and extension states as of July 2005:

Application for a patent before the European Patent Office, either directly or through the PCT pathway, can lead to the processing of the application and, if granted, to a patent in all EPC member states. After granting, the patent still has to be filed with the respective national offices. The legal force of the patent is attained by the act of granting of the patent by the EPO.

As of May 2005, 30 states are full members of the EPC, all of which are also members of the PCT. Another 6 states are associated within the context of the Extension Agreement. The procedure to receive patents in those states is somewhat different, but most general provisions of the EPC also apply there.

The date of ratification of the EPC or the Extension Agreement indicates from what filing date on a EP filing, or a PCT filing naming EP as a designated office, includes the respective country or can be extended to the respective state.

AT	Austria	EE	Estonia
IS	Iceland	PL	Poland
BE	Belgium	ES	Spain
IT	Italy	PT	Portugal
BG	Bulgaria	FI	Finland
LI	Liechtenstein	RO	Romania
CH	Switzerland	FR	France
LT	Lithuania	SE	Sweden
CY	Cyprus	GB	United Kingdom
LU	Luxembourg	SI	Slovenia
CZ	Czech Republic	GR	Hellenic Republic
LV	Latvia	SK	Slovakia
DE	Germany	HU	Hungary
MC	Monaco	TR	Turkey
DK	Denmark	IE	Ireland
NL	Netherlands		

Extension States

AL	Albania	YU	Serbia and Montenegro
BA	Bosnia and Herzegovina		(formerly known as the Federal
HR	Croatia		Republic of Yugoslavia)
MK	former Yugoslav Republic of Macedonia		

For updates see: www.european-patent-office.org/epo/members.htm

Annex 4
Nice Classification of goods and services (8th edition) –
Headings Goods and Services

Class 1   Chemicals used in industry, science and photography, as well as in agriculture, horticulture and forestry; unprocessed artificial resins, unprocessed plastics; manures; fire extinguishing compositions; tempering and soldering preparations; chemical substances for preserving foodstuffs; tanning substances; adhesives used in industry.

Class 2   Paints, varnishes, lacquers; preservatives against rust and against deterioration of wood; colorants; mordants; raw natural resins; metals in foil and powder form for painters, decorators, printers and artists.

Class 3   Bleaching preparations and other substances for laundry use; cleaning, polishing, scouring and abrasive preparations; soaps; perfumery, essential oils, cosmetics, hair lotions; dentifrices.

Class 4   Industrial oils and greases; lubricants; dust absorbing, wetting and binding compositions; fuels (including motor spirit) and illuminants; candles and wicks for lighting.

Class 5   Pharmaceutical and veterinary preparations; sanitary preparations for medical purposes; dietetic substances adapted for medical use, food for babies; plasters, materials for dressings; material for stopping teeth, dental wax; disinfectants; preparations for destroying vermin; fungicides, herbicides.

Class 6   Common metals and their alloys; metal building materials; transportable buildings of metal; materials of metal for railway tracks; non-electric cables and wires of common metal; ironmongery, small items of metal hardware; pipes and tubes of metal; safes; goods of common metal not included in other classes; ores.

Class 7   Machines and machine tools; motors and engines (except for land vehicles); machine coupling and transmission components (except for land vehicles); agricultural implements other than hand-operated; incubators for eggs.

Class 8   Hand tools and implements (hand-operated); cutlery; side arms; razors.

Class 9   Scientific, nautical, surveying, photographic, cinematographic, optical, weighing, measuring, signaling, checking (supervision), life-saving and teaching apparatus and instruments; apparatus and instruments for conducting, switching, transforming, accumulating, regulating or controlling electricity; apparatus for recording, transmission or reproduction of sound or images; magnetic data carriers, recording discs; automatic vending machines and mechanisms for coin-operated apparatus; cash registers, calculating machines, data processing equipment and computers; fire-extinguishing apparatus.

Class 10   Surgical, medical, dental and veterinary apparatus and instruments, artificial limbs, eyes and teeth; orthopedic articles; suture materials.

Class 11	Apparatus for lighting, heating, steam generating, cooking, refrigerating, drying, ventilating, water supply and sanitary purposes.
Class 12	Vehicles; apparatus for locomotion by land, air or water.
Class 13	Firearms; ammunition and projectiles; explosives; fireworks.
Class 14	Precious metals and their alloys and goods in precious metals or coated therewith, not included in other classes; jewellery, precious stones; horological and chronometric instruments.
Class 15	Musical instruments.
Class 16	Paper, cardboard and goods made from these materials, not included in other classes; printed matter; bookbinding material; photographs; stationery; adhesives for stationery or household purposes; artists' materials; paint brushes; typewriters and office requisites (except furniture); instructional and teaching material (except apparatus); plastic materials for packaging (not included in other classes); printers' type; printing blocks.
Class 17	Rubber, gutta-percha, gum, asbestos, mica and goods made from these materials and not included in other classes; plastics in extruded form for use in manufacture; packing, stopping and insulating materials; flexible pipes, not of metal.
Class 18	Leather and imitations of leather, and goods made of these materials and not included in other classes; animal skins, hides; trunks and traveling bags; umbrellas, parasols and walking sticks; whips, harness and saddlery.
Class 19	Building materials (non-metallic); non-metallic rigid pipes for building; asphalt, pitch and bitumen; non-metallic transportable buildings; monuments, not of metal.
Class 20	Furniture, mirrors, picture frames; goods (not included in other classes) of wood, cork, reed, cane, wicker, horn, bone, ivory, whalebone, shell, amber, mother-of-pearl, meerschaum and substitutes for all these materials, or of plastics.
Class 21	Household or kitchen utensils and containers (not of precious metal or coated therewith); combs and sponges; brushes (except paint brushes); brush-making materials; articles for cleaning purposes; steelwool; unworked or semi-worked glass (except glass used in building); glassware, porcelain and earthenware not included in other classes.
Class 22	Ropes, string, nets, tents, awnings, tarpaulins, sails, sacks and bags (not included in other classes); padding and stuffing materials (except of rubber or plastics); raw fibrous textile materials.
Class 23	Yarns and threads, for textile use.
Class 24	Textiles and textile goods, not included in other classes; bed and table covers.
Class 25	Clothing, footwear, headgear.
Class 26	Lace and embroidery, ribbons and braid; buttons, hooks and eyes, pins and needles; artificial flowers.

Class 27 Carpets, rugs, mats and matting, linoleum and other materials for covering existing floors; wall hangings (non-textile).

Class 28 Games and playthings; gymnastic and sporting articles not included in other classes; decorations for Christmas trees.

Class 29 Meat, fish, poultry and game; meat extracts; preserved, dried and cooked fruits and vegetables; jellies, jams, compotes; eggs, milk and milk products; edible oils and fats.

Class 30 Coffee, tea, cocoa, sugar, rice, tapioca, sago, artificial coffee; flour and preparations made from cereals, bread, pastry and confectionery, ices; honey, treacle; yeast, baking-powder; salt, mustard; vinegar, sauces (condiments); spices; ice.

Class 31 Agricultural, horticultural and forestry products and grains not included in other classes; live animals; fresh fruits and vegetables; seeds, natural plants and flowers; foodstuffs for animals, malt.

Class 32 Beers; mineral and aerated waters and other non-alcoholic drinks; fruit drinks and fruit juices; syrups and other preparations for making beverages.

Class 33 Alcoholic beverages (except beers).

Class 34 Tobacco; smokers' articles; matches

Class 35 Advertising; business management; business administration; office functions.

Class 36 Insurance; financial affairs; monetary affairs; real estate affairs.

Class 37 Building construction; repair; installation services.

Class 38 Telecommunications.

Class 39 Transport; packaging and storage of goods; travel arrangement.

Class 40 Treatment of materials.

Class 41 Education; providing of training; entertainment; sporting and cultural activities.

Class 42 Scientific and technological services and research and design relating thereto; industrial analysis and research services; design and development of computer hardware and software; legal services.

Class 43 Services for providing food and drink; temporary accommodation.

Class 44 Medical services; veterinary services; hygienic and beauty care for human beings or animals; agriculture, horticulture and forestry services.

Class 45 Personal and social services rendered by others to meet the needs of individuals; security services for the protection of property and individuals.

Annex 5
International Classification for Industrial Designs under the Locarno Agreement –
Headings Goods and Services

Class 1   Foodstuffs
Class 2   Articles of clothing and haberdashery
Class 3   Travel goods, cases, parasols and personal belongings, not elsewhere
              specified
Class 4   Brush ware
Class 5   Textile piece goods, artificial and natural sheet material
Class 6   Furnishing
Class 7   Household goods, not elsewhere specified
Class 8   Tools and hardware
Class 9   Packages and containers for the transport or handling of goods
Class 10   Clocks and watches and other measuring instruments, checking and
              signaling instruments
Class 11   Articles of adornment
Class 12   Means of transport or hoisting
Class 13   Equipment for production, distribution or transformation of electricity
Class 14   Recording, communication or information retrieval equipment
Class 15   Machines, not elsewhere specified
Class 16   Photographic, cinematographic and optical apparatus
Class 17   Musical instruments
Class 18   Printing and office machinery
Class 19   Stationery and office equipment, artists' and teaching materials
Class 20   Sales and advertising equipment, signs
Class 21   Games, toys, tents and sports goods
Class 22   Arms, pyrotechnic articles, articles for hunting, fishing and pest killing
Class 23   Fluid distribution equipment, sanitary, heating, ventilation and air-con-
              ditioning equipment, solid fuel
Class 24   Medical and laboratory equipment
Class 25   Building units and construction elements
Class 26   Lighting apparatus
Class 27   Tobacco and smokers' supplies
Class 28   Pharmaceutical and cosmetic products, toilet articles and apparatus
Class 29   Devices and equipment against fire hazards, for accident prevention
              and for rescue
Class 30   Articles for the care and handling of animals
Class 31   Machines and appliances for preparing food or drink not elsewhere
              specified
Class 99   Miscellaneous

Annex 6
European Community Member States

European Community Member States (25 countries since May 1st, 2004): Austria, Belgium, Cyprus, Czech Republic, Denmark, Estonia, Finland, France, Germany, Greece, Hungary, Ireland, Italy, Latvia, Lithuania, Luxembourg, Malta, Poland, Portugal, Slovakia, Slovenia, Spain, Sweden, The Netherlands, United Kingdom.

Annex 7
Member countries of the Madrid Agreement and Madrid Protocol

Member countries of the Madrid Agreement and Madrid Protocol as of July 15, 2004: Albania, Algeria, Antigua and Barbuda, Armenia, Australia, Austria, Azerbaijan, Belarus, Bhutan, Bosnia and Herzegovina, Benelux (Belgium, Luxembourg, Netherlands: under the Madrid System, protection shall be requested as if they were one country), Bulgaria, China, Croatia, Cuba, Cyprus, Czech Republic, Democratic People's Republic of Korea, Denmark, Egypt, Estonia, European Community, Finland, France, Georgia, Germany, Greece, Hungary, Iceland, Iran (Islamic Republic of), Ireland, Italy, Japan, Kazakhstan, Kenya, Kyrgyzstan, Latvia, Lesotho, Liberia, Liechtenstein, Lithuania, Monaco, Mongolia, Morocco, Mozambique, Namibia, Norway, Poland, Portugal, Republic of Korea, Republic of Moldova, Romania, Russian Federation, San Marino, Serbia and Montenegro, Sierra Leone, Singapore, Slovakia, Slovenia, Spain, Sudan, Swaziland, Sweden, Switzerland, Syrian Arab Republic, Tajikistan, The former Yugoslav Republic of Macedonia, Turkey, Turkmenistan, Ukraine, United Kingdom, United States of America, Uzbekistan, Viet Nam, Zambia.

For updates see www.wipo.int/madrid

Annex 8
ARIPO member states

ARIPO member states as of July 2005: Botswana, Gambia, Ghana, Kenya, Lesotho, Malawi, Mozambique, Sierra Leone, Somalia, Sudan, Swaziland, Tanzania, Uganda, Zambia and Zimbabwe.

Further, ARIPO cooperates with several non member states who are potential member states with observer status: Angola, Egypt, Eritrea, Ethiopia, Liberia, Mauritius, Namibia, Nigeria, Seychelles and South Africa

For updates see www.aripo.wipo.net

Annex 9
OAPI member states

OAPI (African Intellectual Property Organisation) member states: Benin, Burkina-Faso, Cameroon, Central African Republic, Chad, Congo, Equatorial Guinea, Gabon, Guinea, Guinea-Bissau, Côte d'Ivoire, Mali, Mauritania, Niger, Senegal, Togo

For updates see www.oapi.wipo.net

Annex 10
Order of country codes
(Situation at 9. 3. 2005)

Code[1]	Country	Code[1]	Country
AD	Andorra	BW	Botswana
AE	United Arab Emirates	BY	Belarus
AF	Afghanistan	BZ	Belize
AG	Antigua and Barbuda	CA	Canada
AL	Albania	CD	Democratic Republic of the Congo
AM	Armenia		
AO	Angola	CF	Central African Republic
AR	Argentina	CG	Congo
AT	Austria	CH	Switzerland
AU	Australia	CI	Côte d'Ivoire
AX	Åland Islands	CK	Cook Islands
AZ	Azerbaijan	CL	Chile
BA	Bosnia and Herzegovina	CM	Cameroon
BB	Barbados	CN	China
BD	Bangladesh	CO	Colombia
BE	Belgium	CR	Costa Rica
BF	Burkina Faso	CS	Serbia and Montenegro[2]
BG	Bulgaria	CU	Cuba
BH	Bahrain	CV	Cape Verde
BI	Burundi	CY	Cyprus
BJ	Benin	CZ	Czech Republic
BN	Brunei	DE	Germany
BO	Bolivia	DJ	Djibouti
BR	Brazil	DK	Denmark
BS	The Bahamas	DM	Dominica
BT	Bhutan	DO	Dominican Republic

Code[1]	Country	Code[1]	Country
DZ	Algeria	KN	Saint Kitts and Nevis
EC	Ecuador	KP	North Korea
EE	Estonia	KR	South Korea
EG	Egypt	KW	Kuwait
EL	Greece	KZ	Kazakhstan
ER	Eritrea	LA	Laos
ES	Spain	LB	Lebanon
ET	Ethiopia	LC	Saint Lucia
FI	Finland	LI	Liechtenstein
FJ	Fiji	LK	Sri Lanka
FM	Micronesia	LR	Liberia
FR	France	LS	Lesotho
GA	Gabon	LT	Lithuania
GD	Grenada	LU	Luxembourg
GE	Georgia	LV	Latvia
GH	Ghana	LY	Libya
GM	The Gambia	MA	Morocco
GN	Guinea	MC	Monaco
GQ	Equatorial Guinea	MD	Moldova
GT	Guatemala	MG	Madagascar
GW	Guinea-Bissau	MH	Marshall Islands
GY	Guyana	MK[3]	Former Yugoslav Republic of Macedonia
HN	Honduras		
HR	Croatia	ML	Mali
HT	Haiti	MM	Myanmar
HU	Hungary	MN	Mongolia
ID	Indonesia	MR	Mauritania
IE	Ireland	MT	Malta
IL	Israel	MU	Mauritius
IN	India	MV	Maldives
IQ	Iraq	MW	Malawi
IR	Iran	MX	Mexico
IS	Iceland	MY	Malaysia
IT	Italy	MZ	Mozambique
JM	Jamaica	NA	Namibia
JO	Jordan	NE	Niger
JP	Japan	NG	Nigeria
KE	Kenya	NI	Nicaragua
KG	Kyrgyzstan	NL	Netherlands
KH	Cambodia	NO	Norway
KI	Kiribati	NP	Nepal
KM	The Comoros	NR	Nauru

Code[1]	Country	Code[1]	Country
NU	Niue	SZ	Swaziland
NZ	New Zealand	TD	Chad
OM	Oman	TG	Togo
PA	Panama	TH	Thailand
PE	Peru	TJ	Tajikistan
PG	Papua New Guinea	TL	East Timor
PH	Philippines	TM	Turkmenistan
PK	Pakistan	TN	Tunisia
PL	Poland	TO	Tonga
PT	Portugal	TR	Turkey
PW	Palau	TT	Trinidad and Tobago
PY	Paraguay	TV	Tuvalu
QA	Qatar	TW	Taiwan
RO	Romania	TZ	Tanzania
RU	Russia	UA	Ukraine
RW	Rwanda	UG	Uganda
SA	Saudi Arabia	UK	United Kingdom
SB	Solomon Islands	US	United States
SC	Seychelles	UY	Uruguay
SD	Sudan	UZ	Uzbekistan
SE	Sweden	VA	Holy See/Vatican City
SG	Singapore	VC	Saint Vincent and the
SI	Slovenia		Grenadines
SK	Slovakia	VE	Venezuela
SL	Sierra Leone	VN	Vietnam
SM	San Marino	VU	Vanuatu
SN	Senegal	WS	Western Samoa
SO	Somalia	YE	Yemen
SR	Suriname	ZA	South Africa
ST	Sâo Tomé and Príncipe	ZM	Zambia
SV	El Salvador	ZW	Zimbabwe
SY	Syria		

[1] For the classification of principal currency codes, see point 7.1. See also Annex A5 for names of countries.

[2] At the first mention of 'Serbia and Montenegro' or the ISO code 'CS', the following note is to be added: 'Including Kosovo, under the auspices of the United Nations, pursuant to UN Security Council Resolution 1244 of 10 June 1999.'

[3] The ISO code (MK) is accepted from now on, subject to addition of the following note: 'Provisional code which does not prejudge in any way the definitive nomenclature for this country, which will be agreed following the conclusion of negotiations currently taking place on this subject at the United Nations.'

Index

Intellectual Property Management. Claas Junghans, Adam Levy
Copyright © 2006 WILEY-VCH Verlag GmbH & Co. KGaA, Weinheim